W9-AXK-107

Shakespeare
Explained

As You Like It

CORINNE J. NADEN
INTRODUCTION BY JOSEPH SOBRAN

mc **Marshall Cavendish**
Benchmark
New York

Consultant: Richard Larkin

Published by Marshall Cavendish Benchmark
An imprint of Marshall Cavendish Corporation

Other Marshall Cavendish Offices:
Marshall Cavendish International (Asia) Private Limited, 1 New Industrial Road, Singapore 536196 • Marshall
Cavendish International (Thailand) Co Ltd. 253 Asoke, 12th Flr, Sukhumvit 21 Road, Klongtoey Nua, Wattana,
Bangkok 10110, Thailand • Marshall Cavendish (Malaysia) Sdn Bhd, Times Subang, Lot 46, Subang Hi-Tech
Industrial Park, Batu Tiga, 40000 Shah Alam, Selangor Darul Ehsan, Malaysia

Marshall Cavendish is a trademark of Times Publishing Limited
All websites were available and accurate when this book was sent to press.

Library of Congress Cataloguing-in-Publication Data
Naden, Corinne J.
As you like it / by Corinne J. Naden ; introduction by Joseph Sobran.
p. cm. — (Shakespeare explained)
Includes bibliographical references and index.
Summary: "A literary analysis of the play 'As You Like It.' Includes information on the history and culture of
Elizabethan England"—Provided by publisher.
ISBN 978-1-60870-015-8
1. Shakespeare, William, 1564-1616. As you like it. I. Title.
PR2803.N33 2011
822.3'3—dc22
2009035466

Photo research by: Linda Sykes
PictureHouse/The Everett Collection: front cover; Eric Gevaert/Shutterstock: 1; Mikhali/Shutterstock: 2-3;
Neven Mendrila/Shutterstock: 3; Raciro/istockphoto: 4, 40, 46, 90; Art Parts RF: 6, 8, 13, 26, 27, 34, back cover;
©Nik Wheeler/Corbis: 11; Portraitgalerie, Schloss Ambras, Innsbruck, Austria/Erich Lessing/Art Resource, NY:
20; Travelshots.com/Alamy: 22; ©Hideo Kurihara/Alamy: 24; Corbis/Sygma: 29; Andrew Fox/Corbis: 32; The
Everett Collection: 39; ©Lions Gate Films, Lions Gate Entertainment: 45; ©2005 Royal Shakespeare Company:
49; photo by Walter Garschagen/Hudson Valley Shakespeare Festival: 57; Stan Berouh: 64; photo by Walter
Garschagen/Hudson Valley Shakespeare Festival: 73; ©2005 Royal Shakespeare Company: 79; Stan Berouh:
85; Chris Hopkins/British Shakespeare Festival: 89; photo by Walter Garschagen/Hudson Valley Shakespeare
Festival: 93; Hulton Archive/Getty Images: 97.

Editor: Megan Comerford
Publisher: Michelle Bisson
Art Director: Anahid Hamparian
Series Design: Kay Petronio

Printed in Malaysia (T)
135642

Contents

SHAKESPEARE AND HIS WORLD
BY JOSEPH SOBRAN . . . 4

1. SHAKESPEARE AND
AS YOU LIKE IT . . . 38

2. THE PLAY'S THE THING . . . 44

3. A CLOSER LOOK . . . 88

CHRONOLOGY . . . 112

SOURCE NOTES . . . 114

GLOSSARY . . . 116

SUGGESTED ESSAY TOPICS . . . 119

TESTING YOUR MEMORY . . . 120

FURTHER INFORMATION . . . 122

BIBLIOGRAPHY . . . 123

INDEX . . . 124

Shakespeare and His World

WILLIAM SHAKESPEARE, OFTEN NICKNAMED "THE BARD," IS, BEYOND ANY COMPARISON, THE MOST TOWERING NAME IN ENGLISH LITERATURE. MANY CONSIDER HIS PLAYS THE GREATEST EVER WRITTEN. HE STANDS OUT EVEN AMONG GENIUSES.

Yet the Bard is also closer to our hearts than lesser writers, and his tremendous reputation should neither intimidate us nor prevent us from enjoying the simple delights he offers in such abundance. It is as if he had written for each of us personally. As he himself put it, "One touch of nature makes the whole world kin."

Such tragedies as *Hamlet*, *Romeo and Juliet*, and *Macbeth* are world famous, still performed onstage and in films. These and other plays have also been adapted for radio, television, opera, ballet, pantomime, novels, comic books, and other media. Two of the best ways to become familiar with them are to watch some of the many fine movies that have been made of them and to listen to recordings of them by some of the world's great actors.

Even Shakespeare's individual characters have lives of their own, like real historical figures. Hamlet is still regarded as the most challenging role ever written for an actor. Roughly as many whole books have been written about Hamlet, an imaginary character, as about actual historical figures such as Abraham Lincoln and Napoleon Bonaparte.

Shakespeare created an amazing variety of vivid characters. One of Shakespeare's most peculiar traits was that he loved his characters so much—even some of his villains and secondary or comic characters—that at times he let them run away with the play, stealing attention from his heroes and heroines.

So in *A Midsummer Night's Dream* audiences remember the absurd and lovable fool Bottom the Weaver better than the lovers who are the main characters. Romeo's friend Mercutio is more fiery and witty than Romeo himself; legend claims that Shakespeare said he had to kill Mercutio or Mercutio would have killed the play.

Shakespeare also wrote dozens of comedies and historical plays, as well as nondramatic poems. Although his tragedies are now regarded as his greatest works, he freely mixed them with comedy and history. And his sonnets are among the supreme love poems in the English language.

It is Shakespeare's mastery of the English language that keeps his words familiar to us today. Every literate person knows dramatic lines such as "Wherefore art thou Romeo?"; "My kingdom for a horse!"; "To be or not to be: that is the question"; "Friends, Romans, countrymen, lend me your ears"; and "What fools these mortals be!" Shakespeare's sonnets are noted for their sweetness: "Shall I compare thee to a summer's day?"

LEAVE ME ALONE TO WOO HIM.

SHAKESPEARE'S LANGUAGE

WITHOUT A DOUBT, SHAKESPEARE WAS THE GREATEST MASTER OF THE ENGLISH LANGUAGE WHO EVER LIVED. BUT JUST WHAT DOES THAT MEAN?

Shakespeare's vocabulary was huge, full of references to the Bible as well as Greek and Roman mythology. Yet his most brilliant phrases often combine very simple and familiar words:

"WHAT'S IN A NAME? THAT WHICH WE CALL A ROSE BY ANY OTHER NAME WOULD SMELL AS SWEET."

He has delighted countless millions of readers. And we know him only through his language. He has shaped modern English far more than any other writer.

Or, to put it in more personal terms, you probably quote his words several times every day without realizing it, even if you have never suspected that Shakespeare could be a source of pleasure to you.

So why do so many English-speaking readers find his language so difficult? It is our language, too, but it has changed so much that it is no longer quite the same language—nor a completely different one, either.

Shakespeare's English and ours overlap without being identical. He would have some difficulty understanding us, too! Many of our everyday words and phrases would baffle him.

Shakespeare, for example, would not know what we meant by a *car,* a *radio,* a *movie,* a *television,* a *computer,* or a *sitcom,* since these things did not even exist in his time. Our old-fashioned term *railroad train* would be unimaginable to him, far in the distant future. We would have to explain to him (if we could) what *nuclear weapons, electricity,* and *democracy* are. He would also be a little puzzled by common expressions such as *high-tech, feel the heat, approval ratings, war criminal, judgmental,* and *whoopee cushion.*

So how can we call him "the greatest master of the English language"? It might seem as if he barely spoke English at all! (He would, however, recognize much of our dirty slang, even if he pronounced it slightly differently. His plays also contain many racial insults to Jews, Africans, Italians, Irish, and others. Today he would be called "insensitive.")

Many of the words of Shakespeare's time have become archaic. Words like *thou, thee, thy, thyself,* and *thine,* which were among the most common words in the language in Shakespeare's day, have all but disappeared today. We simply say *you* for both singular and plural, formal and familiar. Most other modern languages have kept their *thou.*

Sometimes the same words now have different meanings. We are apt to be misled by such simple, familiar words as *kind, wonderful, waste, just,* and *dear,* which he often uses in ways that differ from our usage.

Shakespeare also doesn't always use the words we expect to hear, the words that we ourselves would naturally use. When we might automatically say, "I beg your pardon" or just "Sorry," he might say, "I cry you mercy."

Often a glossary and footnotes will solve all three of these problems for us. But it is most important to bear in mind that Shakespeare was often hard for his first audiences to understand. Even in his own time his rich language was challenging. And this was deliberate. Shakespeare was inventing his own kind of English. It remains unique today.

A child doesn't learn to talk by using a dictionary. Children learn first by sheer immersion. We teach babies by pointing at things and saying their names. Yet the toddler always learns faster than we can teach! Even as babies we are geniuses. Dictionaries can help us later, when we already speak and read the language well (and learn more slowly).

So the best way to learn Shakespeare is not to depend on the footnotes and glossary too much, but instead to be like a baby: just get into the flow of the language. Go to performances of the plays or watch movies of them.

THE LANGUAGE HAS A MAGICAL WAY OF TEACHING ITSELF, IF WE LET IT. THERE IS NO REASON TO FEEL STUPID OR FRUSTRATED WHEN IT DOESN'T COME EASILY.

Hundreds of phrases have entered the English language from *Hamlet* alone, including "to hold, as 'twere, the mirror up to nature"; "murder most foul"; "the thousand natural shocks that flesh is heir to"; "flaming youth"; "a countenance more in sorrow than in anger"; "the play's the thing"; "neither a borrower nor a lender be"; "in my mind's eye"; "something is rotten in the state of Denmark"; "alas, poor Yorick"; and "the lady doth protest too much, methinks."

From other plays we get the phrases "star-crossed lovers"; "what's in a name?"; "we have scotched the snake, not killed it"; "one fell swoop"; "it was Greek to me"; "I come to bury Caesar, not to praise him"; and "the most unkindest cut of all"—all these are among our household words. In fact, Shakespeare even gave us the expression "household words." No wonder his contemporaries marveled at his "fine filed phrase" and swooned at the "mellifluous and honey-tongued Shakespeare."

Shakespeare's words seem to combine music, magic, wisdom, and humor:

"THE COURSE OF TRUE LOVE NEVER DID RUN SMOOTH."

"HE JESTS AT SCARS THAT NEVER FELT A WOUND."

"THE FAULT, DEAR BRUTUS, IS NOT IN OUR STARS, BUT IN OURSELVES, THAT WE ARE UNDERLINGS."

"COWARDS DIE MANY TIMES BEFORE THEIR DEATHS; THE VALIANT NEVER TASTE OF DEATH BUT ONCE."

"NOT THAT I LOVED CAESAR LESS, BUT THAT I LOVED ROME MORE."

"THERE ARE MORE THINGS IN HEAVEN AND EARTH, HORATIO, THAN ARE DREAMT OF IN YOUR PHILOSOPHY."

"BREVITY IS THE SOUL OF WIT."

"THERE'S A DIVINITY THAT SHAPES OUR ENDS, ROUGH-HEW THEM HOW WE WILL."

Four centuries after Shakespeare lived, to speak English is to quote him. His huge vocabulary and linguistic fertility are still astonishing. He has had a powerful effect on all of us, whether we realize it or not. We may wonder how it is even possible for a single human being to say so many memorable things.

Only the King James translation of the Bible, perhaps, has had a more profound and pervasive influence on the English language than Shakespeare. And, of course, the Bible was written by many authors over many centuries, and the King James translation, published in 1611, was the combined effort of many scholars.

EARLY LIFE

So who, exactly, was Shakespeare? Mystery surrounds his life, largely because few records were kept during his time. Some people have even doubted his identity, arguing that the real author of Shakespeare's plays must have been a man of superior formal education and wide experience. In a sense such doubts are a natural and understandable reaction to his rare, almost miraculous powers of expression, but some people feel that the doubts themselves show a lack of respect for the supremely human poet.

Most scholars agree that Shakespeare was born in the town of Stratford-upon-Avon in the county of Warwickshire, England, in April 1564. He was baptized, according to local church records, Gulielmus (William) Shakspere (the name was spelled in several different ways) on April 26 of that year. He was one of several children, most of whom died young.

His father, John Shakespeare (or Shakspere), was a glove maker and, at times, a town official. He was often in debt or being fined for unknown delinquencies, perhaps failure to attend church regularly. It is suspected that John was a recusant (secret and illegal) Catholic, but there is no proof. Many

scholars have found Catholic tendencies in Shakespeare's plays, but whether Shakespeare was Catholic or not we can only guess.

At the time of Shakespeare's birth, England was torn by religious controversy and persecution. The country had left the Roman Catholic Church during the reign of King Henry VIII, who had died in 1547. Two of Henry's children, Edward and Mary, ruled after his death. When his daughter Elizabeth I became queen in 1558, she upheld his claim that the monarch of England was also head of the English Church.

Did William attend the local grammar school? He was probably entitled to, given his father's prominence in Stratford, but again, we face a frustrating absence of proof, and many people of the time learned to read very well without schooling. If he went to the town school, he would also have learned the rudiments of Latin.

We know very little about the first half of William's life. In 1582, when he was eighteen, he married Anne Hathaway, eight years his senior. Their first daughter, Susanna, was born six months later. The following year they had twins, Hamnet and Judith.

At this point William disappears from the records again. By the early 1590s we find "William Shakespeare" in London, a member of the city's leading acting company, called the Lord Chamberlain's Men. Many of Shakespeare's greatest roles, we are told, were first performed by the company's star, Richard Burbage.

Curiously, the first work published under (and identified with) Shakespeare's name was not a play but a long erotic poem, *Venus and Adonis*, in 1593. It was dedicated to the young Earl of Southampton, Henry Wriothesley.

Venus and Adonis was a spectacular success, and Shakespeare was immediately hailed as a major poet. In 1594 he dedicated a longer, more serious poem to Southampton, *The Rape of Lucrece*. It was another hit, and for many years, these two poems were considered Shakespeare's greatest works, despite the popularity of his plays.

TRULY THE TREE YIELDS BAD FRUIT

TODAY MOVIES, NOT LIVE PLAYS, ARE THE MORE POPULAR ART FORM. FORTUNATELY MOST OF SHAKESPEARE'S PLAYS HAVE BEEN FILMED, AND THE BEST OF THESE MOVIES OFFER AN EXCELLENT WAY TO MAKE THE BARD'S ACQUAINTANCE. RECENTLY, KENNETH BRANAGH HAS BECOME A RESPECTED CONVERTER OF SHAKESPEARE'S PLAYS INTO FILM.

As You Like It

One of the earliest screen versions of *As You Like It* is the 1936 film starring Laurence Olivier as Orlando and Elisabeth Bergner as Rosalind. The *New York Times*, in a movie review, praised both the directorial interpretation and the actors' portrayals. British actress Helen Mirren starred in a 1978 BBC production that was filmed entirely outdoors. The most recent film version, directed by renowned Shakespearean actor Kenneth Branagh, aired in 2006 on HBO. Set in nineteenth-century Japan, it is visually stunning and a decent interpretation of the play. It also boasts an impressive supporting cast, including Kevin Kline as Jaques, Alfred Molina as Touchstone, and Romola Garai as Celia.

Hamlet

Hamlet, Shakespeare's most famous play, has been well filmed several times. In 1948 Laurence Olivier won three Academy

Awards—for best picture, best actor, and best director—for his version of the play. The film allowed him to show some of the magnetism that made him famous on the stage. Nobody spoke Shakespeare's lines more thrillingly.

The young Derek Jacobi played Hamlet in a 1980 BBC production of the play, with Patrick Stewart (now best known for *Star Trek: The Next Generation*) as the guilty king. Jacobi, like Olivier, has a gift for speaking the lines freshly; he never seems to be merely reciting the famous and familiar words. But whereas Olivier has animal passion, Jacobi is more intellectual. It is fascinating to compare the ways these two outstanding actors play Shakespeare's most complex character.

Franco Zeffirelli's 1990 *Hamlet*, starring Mel Gibson, is fascinating in a different way. Gibson, of course, is best known as an action hero, and he is not well suited to this supremely witty and introspective role, but Zeffirelli cuts the text drastically, and the result turns *Hamlet* into something that few people would have expected: a short, swiftly moving action movie. Several of the other characters are brilliantly played.

Henry IV, Part One

The 1979 BBC Shakespeare series production does a commendable job in this straightforward approach to the play. Battle scenes are effective despite obvious restrictions in an indoor studio setting. Anthony Quayle gives jovial Falstaff a darker edge, and Tim Pigott-Smith's Hotspur is buoyed by some humor. Jon Finch plays King Henry IV with noble authority, and David Gwillim gives Hal a surprisingly successful transformation from boy prince to heir apparent.

Julius Caesar

No really good movie of *Julius Caesar* exists, but the 1953 film, with Marlon Brando as Mark Antony, will do. James Mason is a thoughtful Brutus, and John Gielgud, then ranked with Laurence Olivier among the greatest Shakespearean actors, plays the villainous Cassius. The film is rather dull, and Brando is out of place in a Roman toga, but it is still worth viewing.

King Lear

In the past century, *King Lear* has been adapted for film approximately fifteen times. Peter Brook directed a bleak 1971 version starring British actor Paul Scofield as Lear. One of the best film versions of *King Lear*, not surprisingly, features Laurence Olivier in the title role. The 1983 British TV version, directed by Michael Elliott, provides a straightforward interpretation of the play, though the visual quality may seem dated to the twenty-first-century viewer. Olivier won an Emmy for Outstanding Lead Actor for his role.

Macbeth

Roman Polanski is best known as a director of thrillers and horror films, so it may seem natural that he should have done his 1971 *The Tragedy of Macbeth* as an often-gruesome slasher flick. But this is also one of the most vigorous of all Shakespeare films. Macbeth and his wife are played by Jon Finch and Francesca Annis, neither known for playing Shakespeare, but they are young and attractive in roles that are usually given to older actors, which gives the story a fresh flavor.

The Merchant of Venice

Once again the matchless Sir Laurence Olivier delivers a great performance as Shylock with his wife Joan Plowright as Portia in the 1974 TV film, adapted from the 1970 National Theater (of Britain) production. A 1980 BBC offering features Warren Mitchell as Shylock and Gemma Jones as Portia, with John Rhys-Davies as Salerio. The most recent production, starring Al Pacino as Shylock, Jeremy Irons as Antonio, and Joseph Fiennes as Bassanio, was filmed in Venice and released in 2004.

A Midsummer Night's Dream

Because of the prestige of his tragedies, we tend to forget how many comedies Shakespeare wrote—nearly twice the number of tragedies. Of these perhaps the most popular has always been the enchanting, atmospheric, and very silly masterpiece *A Midsummer Night's Dream*.

Several films have been made of *A Midsummer Night's Dream*. Among the more notable have been Max Reinhardt's 1935 black-and-white version, with Mickey Rooney (then a child star) as Puck.

Of the several film versions, the one starring Kevin Kline as Bottom and Stanley Tucci as Puck, made in 1999 with nineteenth-century costumes and directed by Michael Hoffman, ranks among the finest, and is surely one of the most sumptuous to watch.

Othello

Orson Welles did a budget European version in 1952, now available as a restored DVD. Laurence Olivier's 1965 film performance is predictably remarkable, though it has been said that he would only approach the part by honoring, even emulating, Paul Robeson's definitive interpretation that ran on Broadway in 1943. (Robeson was the first black actor to play Othello, the Moor of Venice, and he did so to critical acclaim, though sadly his performance was never filmed.) Maggie Smith plays a formidable Desdemona opposite Olivier, and her youth and energy will surprise younger audiences who know her only from the *Harry Potter* films. Laurence Fishburne brilliantly portrayed Othello in the 1995 film, costarring with Kenneth Branagh as a surprisingly human Iago, though Irène Jacob's Desdemona was disappointingly weak.

Richard III

Many well-known actors have portrayed the villainous Richard III on film. Of course, Laurence Olivier stepped in to play the role of Richard in a 1955 version he also directed. Director Richard Loncraine chose to set his 1995 film version in Nazi Germany. The movie, which starred Ian McKellen as Richard, was nominated for two Oscars; McKellen was nominated for a Golden Globe for his performance. The World War II interpretation also featured Robert Downey Jr. as Rivers, Kristin Scott Thomas as Lady Anne, and Maggie Smith (from the *Harry Potter* movies) as the Duchess of York. A 2008 version, directed by and starring Scott Anderson, is set in modern-day Los Angeles. Prolific actor David Carradine portrays Buckingham.

Romeo and Juliet

This, the world's most famous love story, has been filmed many times, twice very successfully over the last generation. Franco Zeffirelli directed a hit version in 1968 with Leonard Whiting and the rapturously pretty Olivia Hussey, set in Renaissance Italy. Baz

Luhrmann made a much more contemporary version, with a loud rock score, starring Leonardo DiCaprio and Claire Danes, in 1996.

It seems safe to say that Shakespeare would have preferred Zeffirelli's movie, with its superior acting and rich, romantic, sun-drenched Italian scenery.

The Taming of the Shrew

Franco Zeffirelli's 1967 film version of *The Taming of the Shrew* starred Elizabeth Taylor as Kate and Richard Burton as Petruchio. Shakespeare's original lines were significantly cut and altered to accommodate both the film media and Taylor's inexperience as a Shakespearean actress.

Gil Junger's 1999 movie *10 Things I Hate About You* is loosely based on Shakespeare's play. Julia Stiles and Heath Ledger star in this interpretation set in a modern-day high school. In 2005 BBC aired a version of Shakespeare's play set in twenty-first-century England. Kate is a successful, driven politician who succumbs to cash-strapped Petruchio, played by Rufus Sewell.

The Tempest

A 1960 Hallmark Hall of Fame production featured Maurice Evans as Prospero, Lee Remick as Miranda, Roddy McDowall as Ariel, and Richard Burton as Caliban. The special effects are primitive and the costumes are ludicrous, but it moves along at a fast pace. Another TV version aired in 1998 and was nominated for a Golden Globe. Peter Fonda played Gideon Prosper, and Katherine Heigl played his daughter Miranda Prosper. Sci-fi fans may already know that the classic 1956 film *Forbidden Planet* is modeled on themes and characters from the play.

Twelfth Night

Trevor Nunn adapted the play for the 1996 film he also directed in a rapturous Edwardian setting, with big names like Helena Bonham Carter, Richard E. Grant, Imogen Stubbs, and Ben Kingsley as Feste. A 2003 film set in modern Britain provides an interesting multicultural experience; it features an Anglo-Indian cast with Parminder Nagra (*Bend It Like Beckham*) playing Viola. For the truly intrepid, a twelve-minute silent film made in 1910 does a fine job of capturing the play through visual gags and over-the-top gesturing.

THESE FILMS HAVE BEEN SELECTED FOR SEVERAL QUALITIES: APPEAL AND ACCESSIBILITY TO MODERN AUDIENCES, EXCELLENCE IN ACTING, PACING, VISUAL BEAUTY, AND, OF COURSE, FIDELITY TO SHAKESPEARE. THEY ARE THE MOTION PICTURES WE JUDGE MOST LIKELY TO HELP STUDENTS UNDERSTAND THE SOURCE OF THE BARD'S LASTING POWER.

SHAKESPEARE'S THEATER

Today we sometimes speak of "live entertainment." In Shakespeare's day, of course, all entertainment was live, because recordings, films, television, and radio did not yet exist. Even printed books were a novelty.

In fact, most communication in those days was difficult. Transportation was not only difficult but slow, chiefly by horse and boat. Most people were illiterate peasants who lived on farms that they seldom left; cities grew up along waterways and were subject to frequent plagues that could wipe out much of the population within weeks.

Money—in coin form, not paper—was scarce and hardly existed outside the cities. By today's standards, even the rich were poor. Life

ELIZABETH I, A GREAT PATRON OF POETRY AND THE THEATER, WROTE SONNETS AND TRANSLATED CLASSIC WORKS.

was precarious. Most children died young, and famine or disease might kill anyone at any time. Everyone was familiar with death. Starvation was not rare or remote, as it is to most of us today. Medical care was poor and might kill as many people as it healed.

This was the grim background of Shakespeare's theater during the reign of Queen Elizabeth I, who ruled from 1558 until her death in 1603. During that period England was also torn by religious conflict, often violent, among Roman Catholics who were loyal to the pope, adherents of the Church of England who were loyal to the queen, and the Puritans who would take over the country in the revolution of 1642.

Under these conditions, most forms of entertainment were luxuries that were out of most people's reach. The only way to hear music was to be in the actual physical presence of singers or musicians with their instruments, which were primitive by our standards.

One brutal form of entertainment, popular in London, was bearbaiting. A bear was blinded and chained to a stake, where fierce dogs called mastiffs were turned loose to tear him apart. The theaters had to compete with the bear gardens, as they were called, for spectators.

The Puritans, or radical Protestants, objected to bearbaiting and tried to ban it. Despite their modern reputation, the Puritans were anything but conservative. Conservative people, attached to old customs, hated the Puritans. They seemed to upset everything. (Many of America's first settlers, such as the Pilgrims who came over on the *Mayflower*, were dissidents who were fleeing the Church of England.)

Plays were extremely popular, but they were primitive, too. They had to be performed outdoors in the afternoon because of the lack of indoor lighting. Often the "theater" was only an enclosed courtyard. Probably the versions of Shakespeare's plays that we know today were not used in full, but shortened to about two hours for actual performance.

But eventually more regular theaters were built, featuring a raised stage extending into the audience. Poorer spectators (illiterate "groundlings") stood on the ground around it, at times exposed to rain and snow. Wealthier people sat in raised tiers above. Aside from some costumes, there were few props or special effects and almost no scenery. Much had to be imagined: Whole battles might be represented by a few actors with swords. Thunder might be simulated by rattling a sheet of tin offstage.

The plays were far from realistic and, under the conditions of the time, could hardly try to be. Above the rear of the main stage was a small balcony. (It was this balcony from which Juliet spoke to Romeo.) Ghosts and witches might appear by entering through a trapdoor in the stage floor.

Unlike the modern theater, Shakespeare's Globe Theater—he describes it as "this wooden O"—had no curtain separating the stage from the audience. This allowed intimacy between the players and the spectators.

THE RECONSTRUCTED GLOBE THEATER WAS COMPLETED IN 1997 AND IS LOCATED IN LONDON, JUST 200 YARDS (183 METERS) FROM THE SITE OF THE ORIGINAL.

"SHE'LL FALL IN LOVE WITH MY ANGER."

The spectators probably reacted rowdily to the play, not listening in reverent silence. After all, they had come to have fun! And few of them were scholars. Again, a play had to amuse people who could not read.

The lines of plays were written and spoken in prose or, more often, in a form of verse called iambic pentameter (ten syllables with five stresses per line). There was no attempt at modern realism. Only males were allowed on the stage, so some of the greatest women's roles ever written had to be played by boys or men. (The same is true, by the way, of the ancient Greek theater.)

Actors had to be versatile, skilled not only in acting, but also in fencing, singing, dancing, and acrobatics. Within its limitations, the theater offered a considerable variety of spectacles.

Plays were big business, not yet regarded as high art, sponsored by important and powerful people (the queen loved them as much as the groundlings did). The London acting companies also toured and performed in the provinces. When plagues struck London, the government might order the theaters to be closed to prevent the spread of disease among crowds. (They remained empty for nearly two years from 1593 to 1594.)

As the theater became more popular, the Puritans grew as hostile to it as they were to bearbaiting. Plays, like books, were censored by the government, and the Puritans fought to increase restrictions, eventually banning any mention of God and other sacred topics on the stage.

In 1642 the Puritans shut down all the theaters in London, and in 1644 they had the Globe demolished. The theaters remained closed until Charles's son, King Charles II, was restored to the throne in 1660 and the hated Puritans were finally vanquished.

But, by then, the tradition of Shakespeare's theater had been fatally interrupted. His plays remained popular, but they were often rewritten by inferior dramatists, and it was many years before they were performed (again) as he had originally written them.

THE ROYAL SHAKESPEARE THEATER, IN STRATFORD-UPON-AVON, WAS CLOSED IN 2007 TO BUILD A 1,000-SEAT AUDITORIUM.

SHAKESPEARE EXPLAINED: AS YOU LIKE IT

Today, of course, the plays are performed both in theaters and in films, sometimes in costumes of the period (ancient Rome for *Julius Caesar*, medieval England for *Henry V*), sometimes in modern dress (*Richard III* has recently been reset in England in the 1930s).

PLAYS

In the England of Queen Elizabeth I, plays were enjoyed by all classes of people, but they were not yet respected as a serious form of art.

Shakespeare's plays began to appear in print in individual, or quarto, editions in 1594, but none of these bore his name until 1598. Although his tragedies are now ranked as his supreme achievements, his name was first associated with comedies and with plays about English history.

The dates of Shakespeare's plays are notoriously hard to determine. Few performances of them were documented; some were not printed until decades after they first appeared on the stage. Mainstream scholars generally place most of the comedies and histories in the 1590s, admitting that this time frame is no more than a widely accepted estimate.

The three parts of *King Henry VI*, culminating in a fourth part, *Richard III*, deal with the long and complex dynastic struggle or civil wars known as the Wars of the Roses (1455–1487), one of England's most turbulent periods. Today it is not easy to follow the plots of these plays.

It may seem strange to us that a young playwright should have written such demanding works early in his career, but they were evidently very popular with the Elizabethan public. Of the four, only *Richard III*, with its wonderfully villainous starring role, is still often performed.

Even today, one of Shakespeare's early comedies, *The Taming of the Shrew*, remains a crowd-pleaser. (It has enjoyed success in a 1999 film adaptation, *10 Things I Hate About You*, with Heath Ledger and Julia Stiles.) The story is simple: The enterprising Petruchio resolves to marry a rich

THE "REAL" SHAKESPEARE

AROUND 1850 DOUBTS STARTED TO SURFACE ABOUT WHO HAD ACTUALLY WRITTEN SHAKESPEARE'S PLAYS, CHIEFLY BECAUSE MANY OTHER AUTHORS, SUCH AS MARK TWAIN, THOUGHT THE PLAYS' AUTHOR WAS TOO WELL EDUCATED AND KNOWLEDGEABLE TO HAVE BEEN THE MODESTLY SCHOOLED MAN FROM STRATFORD.

Who, then, was the real author? Many answers have been given, but the three leading candidates are Francis Bacon, Christopher Marlowe, and Edward de Vere, Earl of Oxford.

Francis Bacon (1561-1626)

Bacon was a distinguished lawyer, scientist, philosopher, and essayist. Many considered him one of the great geniuses of his time, capable of any literary achievement, though he wrote little poetry and, as far as we know, no dramas. When people began to suspect that "Shakespeare" was only a pen name, he seemed like a natural candidate. But his writing style was vastly different from the style of the plays.

Christopher Marlowe (1564–1593)

Marlowe wrote several excellent tragedies in a style much like that of the Shakespearean tragedies, though without the comic blend. But he was reportedly killed in a mysterious incident in 1593, before most of the Bard's plays existed. Could his death have been faked? Is it possible that he lived on for decades in hiding, writing under a pen name? This is what his advocates contend.

Edward de Vere, Earl of Oxford (1550–1604)

Oxford is now the most popular and plausible alternative to the lad from Stratford. He had a high reputation as a poet and playwright in his day, but his life was full of scandal. That controversial life seems to match what the poet says about himself in the sonnets, as well as many events in the plays (especially *Hamlet*). However, he died in 1604, and most scholars believe this rules him out as the author of plays that were published after that date.

THE GREAT MAJORITY OF EXPERTS REJECT THESE AND ALL OTHER ALTERNATIVE CANDIDATES, STICKING WITH THE TRADITIONAL VIEW, AFFIRMED IN THE 1623 FIRST FOLIO OF THE PLAYS, THAT THE AUTHOR WAS THE MAN FROM STRATFORD. THAT REMAINS THE SAFEST POSITION TO TAKE, UNLESS STARTLING NEW EVIDENCE TURNS UP, WHICH, AT THIS LATE DATE, SEEMS HIGHLY UNLIKELY.

young woman, Katherina Minola, for her wealth, despite her reputation for having a bad temper. Nothing she does can discourage this dauntless suitor, and the play ends with Kate becoming a submissive wife. It is all the funnier for being unbelievable.

With *Romeo and Juliet* the Bard created his first enduring triumph. This tragedy of "star-crossed lovers" from feuding families is known around the world. Even people with only the vaguest knowledge of Shakespeare are often aware of this universally beloved story. It has inspired countless similar stories and adaptations, such as the hit musical *West Side Story*.

By the mid-1590s Shakespeare was successful and prosperous, a partner in the Lord Chamberlain's Men. He was rich enough to buy New Place, one of the largest houses in his hometown of Stratford.

Yet, at the peak of his good fortune came the worst sorrow of his life: Hamnet, his only son, died in August 1596 at the age of eleven, leaving nobody to carry on his family name, which was to die out with his two daughters.

Our only evidence of his son's death is a single line in the parish burial register. As far as we know, this crushing loss left no mark on Shakespeare's work. As far as his creative life shows, it was as if nothing had happened. His silence about his grief may be the greatest puzzle of his mysterious life, although, as we shall see, others remain.

During this period, according to traditional dating (even if it must be somewhat hypothetical), came the torrent of Shakespeare's mightiest works. Among these was another quartet of English history plays, this one centering on the legendary King Henry IV, including *Richard II* and the two parts of *Henry IV*.

Then came a series of wonderful romantic comedies: *Much Ado About Nothing*, *As You Like It*, and *Twelfth Night*.

In 1598 the clergyman Francis Meres, as part of a larger work, hailed

ACTOR JOSEPH FIENNES PORTRAYED THE BARD IN THE 1998 FILM *SHAKESPEARE IN LOVE*, DIRECTED BY JOHN MADDEN.

Shakespeare as the English Ovid, supreme in love poetry as well as drama. "The Muses would speak with Shakespeare's fine filed phrase," Meres wrote, "if they would speak English." He added praise of Shakespeare's "sugared sonnets among his private friends." It is tantalizing; Meres seems to know something of the poet's personal life, but he gives us no hard information. No wonder biographers are frustrated.

Next the Bard returned gloriously to tragedy with *Julius Caesar*. In the play Caesar has returned to Rome in great popularity after his military triumphs. Brutus and several other leading senators, suspecting that Caesar means to make himself king, plot to assassinate him. Midway through the play, after the assassination, comes one of Shakespeare's most famous scenes. Brutus speaks at Caesar's funeral. But then Caesar's friend Mark Antony delivers a powerful attack on the conspirators, inciting the mob to fury. Brutus and the others, forced to flee Rome, die in the ensuing civil war. In the end the spirit of Caesar wins after all. If Shakespeare had written nothing after *Julius Caesar*, he would still have been remembered as one of the greatest playwrights of all time. But his supreme works were still to come.

Only Shakespeare could have surpassed *Julius Caesar*, and he did so with *Hamlet* (usually dated about 1600). King Hamlet of Denmark has died, apparently bitten by a poisonous snake. Claudius, his brother, has married the dead king's widow, Gertrude, and become the new king, to the disgust and horror of Prince Hamlet. The ghost of old Hamlet appears to young Hamlet, reveals that he was actually poisoned by Claudius, and demands revenge. Hamlet accepts this as his duty, but cannot bring himself to kill his hated uncle. What follows is Shakespeare's most brilliant and controversial plot.

The story of *Hamlet* is set against the religious controversies of the Bard's time. Is the ghost in hell or purgatory? Is Hamlet Catholic or Protestant? Can revenge ever be justified? We are never really given the answers to such questions. But the play reverberates with them.

THE KING'S MEN

In 1603 Queen Elizabeth I died, and King James VI of Scotland became King James I of England. He also became the patron of Shakespeare's acting company, so the Lord Chamberlain's Men became the King's Men. From this point on, we know less of Shakespeare's life in London than in Stratford, where he kept acquiring property.

In the later years of the sixteenth century Shakespeare had been a rather elusive figure in London, delinquent in paying taxes. From 1602 to 1604 he lived, according to his own later testimony, with a French immigrant family named Mountjoy. After 1604 there is no record of any London residence for Shakespeare, nor do we have any reliable recollection of him or his whereabouts by others. As always, the documents leave much to be desired.

Nearly as great as *Hamlet* is *Othello*, and many regard *King Lear*, the heartbreaking tragedy about an old king and his three daughters, as Shakespeare's supreme tragedy. Shakespeare's shortest tragedy, *Macbeth*, tells the story of a Scottish lord and his wife who plot to murder the king of Scotland to gain the throne for themselves. *Antony and Cleopatra*, a sequel to *Julius Caesar*, depicts the aging Mark Antony in love with the enchanting queen of Egypt. *Coriolanus*, another Roman tragedy, is the poet's least popular masterpiece.

SONNETS AND THE END

The year 1609 saw the publication of Shakespeare's Sonnets. Of these 154 puzzling love poems, the first 126 are addressed to a handsome young man, unnamed, but widely believed to be the Earl of Southampton; the rest concern a dark woman, also unidentified. These mysteries are still debated by scholars.

Near the end of his career Shakespeare turned to comedy again, but it was a comedy of a new and more serious kind. Magic plays a large role in these late plays. For example, in *The Tempest*, the exiled duke of Milan, Prospero, uses magic to defeat his enemies and bring about a final reconciliation.

According to the most commonly accepted view, Shakespeare, not yet fifty, retired to Stratford around 1610. He died prosperous in 1616 and left a will that divided his goods, with a famous provision leaving his wife "my second-best bed." He was buried in the chancel of the parish church, under a tombstone bearing a crude rhyme:

> GOOD FRIEND, FOR JESUS SAKE FORBEARE,
> TO DIG THE DUST ENCLOSED HERE.
> BLEST BE THE MAN THAT SPARES THESE STONES,
> AND CURSED BE HE THAT MOVES MY BONES.

This epitaph is another hotly debated mystery: did the great poet actually compose these lines himself?

SHAKESPEARE'S GRAVE IN HOLY TRINITY CHURCH, STRATFORD-UPON-AVON. HIS WIFE, ANNE HATHAWAY, IS BURIED BESIDE HIM.

THE FOLIO

In 1623 Shakespeare's colleagues of the King's Men produced a large volume of the plays (excluding the sonnets and other poems) titled *Mr. William Shakespeares Comedies, Histories, & Tragedies* with a woodcut portrait of the Bard. As a literary monument it is priceless, containing our only texts of half the plays; as a source of biographical information it is severely disappointing, giving not even the dates of Shakespeare's birth and death.

Ben Jonson, then England's poet laureate, supplied a long prefatory poem saluting Shakespeare as the equal of the great classical Greek tragedians Aeschylus, Sophocles, and Euripides, adding that "He was not of an age, but for all time."

Some would later denigrate Shakespeare. His reputation took more than a century to conquer Europe, where many regarded him as semi-barbarous. His works were not translated before 1740. Jonson himself, despite his personal affection, would deprecate "idolatry" of the Bard. For a time Jonson himself was considered more "correct" than Shakespeare, and possibly the superior artist.

But Jonson's generous verdict is now the whole world's. Shakespeare was not merely of his own age, "but for all time."

"THAT FLATTERING TONGUE OF YOURS WON ME."

allegory—a story in which characters and events stand for general moral truths. Shakespeare never uses this form simply, but his plays are full of allegorical elements.

alliteration—repetition of one or more initial sounds, especially consonants, as in the saying "through thick and thin," or in Julius Caesar's statement, "veni, vidi, vici."

allusion—a reference, especially when the subject referred to is not actually named, but is unmistakably hinted at.

aside—a short speech in which a character speaks to the audience, unheard by other characters on the stage.

comedy—a story written to amuse, using devices such as witty dialogue (high comedy) or silly physical movement (low comedy). Most of Shakespeare's comedies were romantic comedies, incorporating lovers who endure separations, misunderstandings, and other obstacles but who are finally united in a happy resolution.

deus ex machina—an unexpected, artificial resolution to a play's convoluted plot. Literally, "god out of a machine."

dialogue—speech that takes place among two or more characters.

diction—choice of words for a given tone. A speech's diction may be dignified (as when a king formally addresses his court), comic (as when the ignorant grave diggers debate whether Ophelia deserves a religious funeral), vulgar, romantic, or whatever the dramatic occasion requires. Shakespeare was a master of diction.

Elizabethan—having to do with the reign of Queen Elizabeth I, from 1558 until her death in 1603. This is considered the most famous period in the history of England, chiefly because of Shakespeare and other noted authors (among them Sir Philip Sidney, Edmund Spenser, and Christopher Marlowe). It was also an era of military glory, especially the defeat of the huge Spanish Armada in 1588.

Globe—the Globe Theater housed Shakespeare's acting company, the Lord Chamberlain's Men (later known as the King's Men). Built in 1598, it caught fire and burned down during a performance of *Henry VIII* in 1613.

hyperbole—an excessively elaborate exaggeration used to create special emphasis or a comic effect, as in Montague's remark that his son Romeo's sighs are "adding to clouds more clouds" in *Romeo and Juliet.*

irony—a discrepancy between what a character says and what he or she truly believes, what is expected to happen and

what really happens, or what a character says
and what others understand.

metaphor—a figure of speech in which one thing is identified
with another, such as when Hamlet calls his father a "fair
mountain." (See also **simile**.)

monologue—a speech delivered by a single character.

motif—a recurrent theme or image, such as disease in *Hamlet*
or moonlight in *A Midsummer Night's Dream*.

oxymoron—a phrase that combines two contradictory terms, as
in the phrase "sounds of silence" or Hamlet's remark, "I must
be cruel only to be kind."

personification—imparting personality to something impersonal
("the sky wept"); giving human qualities to an idea or an
inanimate object, as in the saying "love is blind."

pun—a playful treatment of words that sound alike, or are
exactly the same, but have different meanings. In *Romeo and
Juliet* Mercutio says, after being fatally wounded, "Ask for
me tomorrow and you shall find me a grave man." *Grave* could
mean either "a place of burial" or "serious."

simile—a figure of speech in which one thing is compared to
another, usually using the word *like* or *as*. (See also **metaphor**.)

soliloquy—a speech delivered by a single character, addressed
to the audience. The most famous are those of Hamlet,
but Shakespeare uses this device frequently to tell us his
characters' inner thoughts.

symbol—a visible thing that stands for an invisible quality, as poison in *Hamlet* stands for evil and treachery.

syntax—sentence structure or grammar. Shakespeare displays amazing variety of syntax, from the sweet simplicity of his songs to the clotted fury of his great tragic heroes, who can be very difficult to understand at a first hearing. These effects are deliberate; if we are confused, it is because Shakespeare means to confuse us.

theme—the abstract subject or message of a work of art, such as revenge in *Hamlet* or overweening ambition in *Macbeth*.

tone—the style or approach of a work of art. The tone of *A Midsummer Night's Dream*, set by the lovers, Bottom's crew, and the fairies, is light and sweet. The tone of *Macbeth*, set by the witches, is dark and sinister.

tragedy—a story that traces a character's fall from power, sanity, or privilege. Shakespeare's well-known tragedies include *Hamlet*, *Macbeth,* and *Othello*.

tragicomedy—a story that combines elements of both tragedy and comedy, moving a heavy plot through twists and turns to a happy ending.

verisimilitude—having the appearance of being real or true.

understatement—a statement expressing less than intended, often with an ironic or comic intention; the opposite of hyperbole.

SHAKESPEARE AND
AS YOU LIKE IT

A movie poster for the 1936 ▶
film version of *As You Like It*,
starring Elisabeth Bergner
and renowned Shakespeare
actor Laurence Olivier.

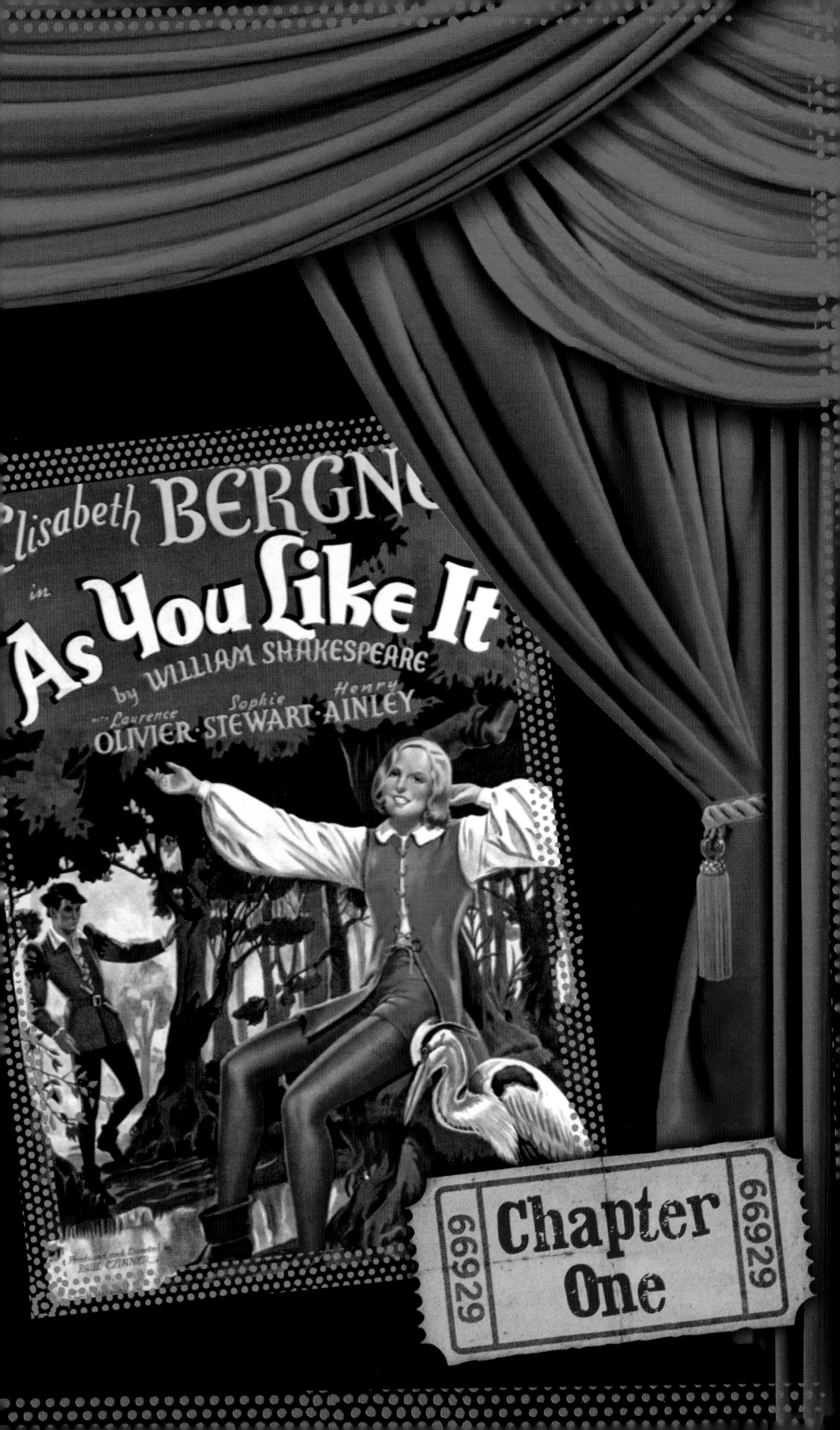

lisabeth BERGN
in
As You Like It
by WILLIAM SHAKESPEARE
with Laurence OLIVIER · Sophie STEWART · Henry AINLEY
669299
Chapter One
669299

Shakespeare and As You Like It

ACCORDING TO MOST SCHOLARS, WILLIAM SHAKESPEARE WROTE A TOTAL OF THIRTY-EIGHT PLAYS. SEVENTEEN ARE GENERALLY CONSIDERED COMEDIES. THAT INCLUDES *AS YOU LIKE IT*, WHICH WAS PROBABLY WRITTEN BETWEEN 1598 AND 1600.

Although there are some earlier references to the play, the first known publication of *As You Like It* appeared in 1623. It was included in an anthology called *Mr. William Shakespeares Comedies, Histories, & Tragedies*, more commonly known as the First Folio. Without it, there would probably be no William Shakespeare because not one of his original manuscripts has survived. In Shakespeare's time, a playwright often gave a draft of his play, called a foul paper, to each actor. Such papers might be copied by a scribe, or copyist, in clear handwriting. The scribe who supposedly copied Shakespeare's plays was Ralph Crane. Scribe copies were given to printers to set type from them.

In the First Folio, *As You Like It* is listed as number ten under Comedies and is marked with an asterisk to signify that it was not published before 1623, approximately seven years after Shakespeare's death. The listing also gives the type of source that was used. For *As You Like It*, the source is "from a quality manuscript, lightly annotated by a prompter."

As You Like It is a pastoral comedy. That means it deals with rustic life and shepherds. (*Pastor* is the Latin word for "shepherd.") In a pastoral comedy, the leisurely rustic background is in sharp contrast to the bustle of court life. In *this* pastoral comedy, most of the action takes place in the country, a forest where the characters have been exiled from a court or city setting. They are now in another world in which the rules of court and society don't seem to apply. Women dress as men, or a nobleman becomes a shepherd. In the end, most of the characters will return to court, their problems solved.

Shakespeare uses the pastoral scene to make fun of social mores both in the city and the country. Life in the Forest of Arden is idealized. Duke Senior, who is banished from court, and his followers may delight in describing rustic life, but they still speak and act as though they were at court. And although Rosalind and Celia play at being shepherd and shepherdess, they never spend any time taking care of sheep; nor do the other minor characters, even those who claim to be shepherds. Chance encounters in the forest and entanglements of various love affairs delight audiences, especially when the productions are staged out of doors in a realistic pastoral setting.

Though there is a lot of talking and not much physical action in the comedy, the dialogue is lively enough to move the plot along quickly. Following pastoral tradition, much discussion, and even song, is devoted to the merits of both city and country backgrounds. In fact, this play contains more singing than any other of Shakespeare's works.

Shakespeare based *As You Like It* on the novel *Rosalynde*, written by Thomas Lodge, probably around 1590. Although Shakespeare was true to the story line, he added several characters: the jester Touchstone, the dull-witted country girl named Audrey, and the melancholy but remarkable Jaques. In Shakespeare's comedies, the two main players usually have a helper who is socially inferior, such as a jester. These helpers are called stock characters. However, in this play the jester Touchstone is not a stock character and is, in fact, one of Shakespeare's most interesting players.

There are two main plots in *As You Like It*. There is the conflict between Orlando and his older brother Oliver, who has inherited their father's estate. There is the conflict between Duke Senior and his younger brother Frederick, who has exiled him. The play also contains four quite different love stories. Unlike the novel, in which Lodge relates the love stories one after the other, Shakespeare presents them all at the same time, giving the characters a chance to make comments on the other couples.

Critics have always been divided about *As You Like It*. Such well-known people as Samuel Johnson and George Bernard Shaw said the play lacked Shakespeare's high artistry. However, there are many who say it is high quality, and entertaining if not groundbreaking. It contains humorous and clever wordplay throughout and improbable chance encounters in the forest. Also included are several—in some cases improbable—love affairs, all with the background of a serene forest setting. In addition, the play contains one of Shakespeare's most often-quoted monologues, which begins, "All the world's a stage" (II.7).

According to tradition, Shakespeare himself played the part of the old servant Adam in the original production of *As You Like It*, which was supposedly performed at the Globe Theater in London in 1599. There is no proof of this, however. The play was more likely first performed in 1603 at Wilton House in Wiltshire, although that date, too, is uncertain.

At the time, King James I and his court were in Wiltshire as guests of William Herbert, third earl of Pembroke. The king had to leave London because of the bubonic plague. (Six outbreaks of the plague over many years reduced the population in London by as much as 30 percent.) On the night of December 2, 1603, a play was staged for the king and his court. According to the Herbert family records, the play was *As You Like It*.

The action in the play is set in the Forest of Arden. Some say Shakespeare was referring to woodlands near his hometown. Others say it depicts the forested region of France and Belgium known as Ardennes, which is a sparsely populated area of dense forests with steep-sided valleys and fast-flowing rivers. The Oxford Shakespeare edition uses the Ardennes spelling, but most other editions of the play use Arden. Interestingly, Shakespeare's mother's name was Mary Arden.

THE PLAY'S THE THING

- OVERVIEW AND ANALYSIS

- LIST OF CHARACTERS

- ANALYSIS OF MAJOR CHARACTERS

A poster for HBO Film's 2007 ▶ version of *As You Like It*. Director Kenneth Branagh set the play in nineteenth-century Japan.

FROM KENNETH BRANAGH,
THE DIRECTOR OF "HENRY V," "HAMLET" AND "MUCH ADO ABOU

WILLIAM SHAKESPEARE'S

AS YOU LIKE IT

ROMANCE OR SOMETHING LIKE IT

ROMOLA   BRYCE DALLAS   KEVIN   ADRIAN   JANET   ALFRED
GARAI   HOWARD   KLINE   LESTER   McTEER   MOLINA

66929   **Chapter Two**   66929

The Play's the Thing

ACT I, SCENE 1

OVERVIEW

In an orchard on the de Boys estate, Orlando talks to Adam, longtime family servant, about his wretched position. When Orlando's father, Sir Roland, died, the family money went to Oliver, the oldest son. This is called primogeniture, an accepted practice of the time. According to their father's wish, it was Oliver's duty to see that his younger brothers got an education befitting a gentleman. However, although Oliver did send brother Jaques off to school, he did not do the same for Orlando, the youngest, who now feels he is treated no better than a peasant.

Oliver enters and the two brothers almost immediately begin fighting. Orlando, the stronger of the two, grabs his brother by the throat. Adam tries to stop the fight. Orlando demands that Oliver treat him like a gentleman or give him the thousand crowns left to him in their father's will. Feeling physically threatened, Oliver agrees to give him money. Then he tells Orlando to get out and says to Adam, "Get you with him, you old dog." Once they leave, Oliver, now suddenly brave, says that he'll cure his brother of his insolence "and yet give no thousand crowns neither."

After they leave, Oliver's servant, Dennis, enters with the news that Charles, the court wrestler, is waiting to see him. Charles enters and reports that Duke Senior, rightful leader of the court, has been banished by his younger brother, Frederick. Duke Senior is now in the Forest of Arden along with some of his faithful lords who volunteered to go into exile with him. Oliver asks if Frederick has also banished Rosalind, Duke Senior's daughter. Charles reports that Rosalind has been allowed to remain at court, mostly due to her close friendship with Celia, Frederick's daughter.

Charles also has another matter on his mind. He is scheduled for a wrestling match the next day. He has learned that Orlando will disguise himself and enter the match. Charles says he does not want to harm the young nobleman, but he has a reputation to uphold. Oliver replies that Orlando is a scoundrel and will use any method to win the match. Thus assured, Charles vows to win: "If he come tomorrow, I'll give him his payment." He leaves, and Oliver is pleased with the thought that his younger brother might be harmed, or even killed, and thus removed from court: "I hope I shall see an end of him; for my soul, yet I know not why, hates nothing more than he."

ANALYSIS

In this short first scene, Shakespeare sets up the two conflicts that make the ensuing events possible: the troubles between two sets of brothers. In one case, younger brother Frederick has wronged older brother Duke

Senior. In the other, older brother Oliver has usurped the rights of younger brother Orlando. In both cases, the brother who has been wronged is morally good.

Oliver's villainy is twofold. In Elizabethan England, primogeniture was a common practice. The eldest son received the bulk of the estate but was bound to carry out the father's will. In this case, it meant educating the other sons. Oliver has refused to educate Orlando. In addition, he encourages the wrestler to inflict harm, even death, upon his brother.

Charles and Orlando represent levels of society that rule life at court. The wrestler assumes he will win the match, but he fears he will be criticized by court society because he has defeated a nobleman, even one as poor as Orlando.

This scene also briefly introduces the contrast between corruption in court life (the treachery of Frederick and Oliver) and the gentleness of life in the Forest of Arden. As Charles says of Duke Senior: "They say he is already in the Forest of Arden, and a many merry men with him; and there they live like the old Robin Hood of England." Charles depicts life in the forest as idyllic by likening Duke Senior to a beloved character from English folklore. Robin Hood, as a fighter against injustice and tyranny, was very popular in Shakespeare's time.

In this scene, and throughout the play, Shakespeare's characters often alternate between formal and informal language. Oliver uses the formal pronoun "you" when he first talks to Charles. However, when he wants to con the wrestler into harming Orlando, he switches to the more familiar pronoun "thou." Shakespeare uses this device often in his works. It helps to establish social levels between characters. By using the familiar pronoun, Oliver attempts to get closer to Charles; in other words, he tries to get the wrestler to do as Oliver wishes.

COURT WRESTLER CHARLES FIGHTS A MASKED
ORLANDO (BARNABY KAY) IN THE ROYAL
SHAKESPEARE COMPANY'S 2005 PRODUCTION,
DIRECTED BY DOMINIC COOKE.

ACT I, SCENE 2

OVERVIEW

Cousins and best friends Rosalind and Celia walk the grounds of Frederick's palace. Celia urges her cousin to be happier, but Rosalind says she grieves for her exiled father, Duke Senior. They are interrupted by Touchstone, the court jester, who says that Celia's father wishes to see her. Soon after, Le Beau, another courtier, joins them with news that the next wrestling match is about to begin. He tells them that Charles has just defeated three opponents, breaking the ribs of one so badly that "there is little hope of life in him."

Frederick asks the young women to persuade the next challenger to withdraw. The newcomer will surely be harmed or killed. Rosalind and Celia do try to dissuade the challenger, who turns out to be Orlando, but he will not listen. In fact, the fight with his brother and the upcoming match appear to have made Orlando melancholy. "Only in the world I fill up a place, which may be better supplied when I have made it empty," he says, suggesting the world might be better off without him.

But to everyone's surprise, Orlando defeats Charles, who has to be carried away. Frederick is stunned by Charles's loss, but becomes angry when he discovers that Orlando is the son of Sir Roland, an old enemy.

Frederick leaves, and Rosalind gives Orlando a chain from her neck to commend his bravery: "Gentleman, / Wear this for me." Rosalind and Orlando are obviously taken with one another. When the two young women depart, Orlando is speechless: "Can I not say I thank you?" He laments that something physically weaker than Charles (the lovely Rosalind) has suddenly taken control of him. Le Beau, returns to warn Orlando of Frederick's anger and its possible consequences. Still in a daze over Rosalind, Orlando decides he had better leave the palace: "Thus must I from the smoke into the smother; / From tyrant duke unto a tyrant brother."

ANALYSIS

This scene introduces the first of many concepts of love in the play. There is the romantic attraction between Orlando and Rosalind. Like many of Shakespeare's lovers, the two instantly fall for one another.

In addition, the two main female characters, Rosalind and Celia, have a very close relationship. In fact, in the first scene Charles says of them: "never two ladies loved as they do." They are cousins, close in age, and have grown up together, so, not surprisingly, the two women are devoted friends. However, to understand their relationship, it is important to realize that certain concepts of love in Elizabethan times were quite different than those of today. A romantic friendship, or one based on nonsexual love, between two people of the same sex was not uncommon. Expressions of such a friendship might involve holding hands or sharing a bed, but that did not indicate a sexual relationship. (In Shakespeare's day it was quite the norm to sleep two in a bed.) Such is the relationship of Rosalind and Celia.

Actually, Elizabethan theater audiences would surely have been much more intrigued with the fact that Rosalind later wears male clothing than with her relationship to Celia. That is because Elizabethan women had little power. They were largely under the control of their fathers and, once they married, of their husbands. There were few ways for women to earn their own money. By donning men's clothes, Rosalind can act in a way not accepted or expected of women. In other words, she frees herself with her disguise.

This scene also introduces Touchstone, the court jester. He is different from the jesters in Shakespeare's earlier works. Those fools were largely stooges and provided slapstick humor. But in Touchstone's case, his humor

"WHAT THINK YOU OF FALLING IN LOVE?"

stems from his intellect and wit. He is at home at court and, when he journeys to Arden, finds himself out of his element because no one there appreciates his sophistication.

ACT I, SCENE 3

OVERVIEW

Back at the palace, Rosalind speaks of her love for Orlando. Celia wants to know how she could have fallen in love so quickly: "is it possible, on such a sudden, you should fall into so strong a liking with old Sir Roland's youngest son?" But their conversation is interrupted by an irate Frederick. He orders Rosalind to leave, threatening, "Within these ten days if that thou be'st found / So near our public court as twenty miles, / Thou diest for it." Rosalind asks for an explanation but is told only that she is her father's daughter.

After Frederick storms off, Rosalind is faced with the fact that she must leave the court. But Celia declares that she will not be separated from Rosalind. The two decide to join Duke Senior in the Forest of Arden. But how can two young women of the court travel safely alone? The answer is disguise. Rosalind will dress as a young man and call herself Ganymede: "Were it not better, / Because that I am more than common tall, / That I did suit me all points like a man?" Celia will dress in "poor and mean attire" to disguise her noble upbringing and will call herself Aliena. Rosalind decides that they would do well to have someone else along. "But, cousin, what if we assay'd to steal / The clownish fool out of your father's court? / Would he not be a comfort to our travel?" Celia assures Rosalind that Touchstone will go with them: "He'll go along o'er the wide world with me."

ANALYSIS

This scene more fully reveals the evil nature of Frederick. He has no reason to banish Rosalind; she has done nothing to him. But, as he says, "Thou art thy father's daughter; / there's enough." His villainy is further evidenced when Celia tells him that if Rosalind is banished from court, she wants the same sentence. She says she cannot live without her cousin, to which her father responds, "You are a fool."

The journey to the forest allows the young girls to don disguises. Characters in disguise was a favorite device in plays of the time, and Shakespeare uses disguise in many of his plays. It added intrigue, mystery, and comedy. Rosalind takes the name of Ganymede, a handsome youth in Greek mythology. In addition, since the actor playing Rosalind was actually a boy, the "disguise" put less of a strain on his talents for most of the play.

The clever inclusion of Touchstone in the journey to Arden has two purposes. Shakespeare endears Touchstone to audiences by casting him as a sort of protector of the two young women. In addition, because he is so clever and witty, he is an excellent commentator on social life in the forest. In Elizabethan times, a touchstone was used to test the purity of gold or silver. The character of Touchstone tests the reality and quality of the play's characters.

ACT II, SCENE 1

OVERVIEW

Surrounded by his loyal lords, Duke Senior talks of his happiness with the quiet life in the Forest of Arden. Everything seems to be perfect and satisfying. However, Duke Senior does lament that they are bound to kill a deer when they go on a hunt. The First Lord tells him that Jaques (who has not yet appeared on stage) bemoans the fate of the deer as well. In fact, according to the lord, Jaques has said that Duke Senior is more guilty for killing a deer than Frederick is for exiling him. When Duke Senior is told that Jaques is now sobbing in the forest over the deer's fate, he asks to see him. He enjoys arguing with the melancholy and sentimental Jaques: "I love to cope him in these sullen fits, / For then he's full of matter."

In this scene, the reader is introduced to the Forest of Arden. Duke Senior extols life there as superior to life at court: "Are not these woods / More free from peril than the envious court?" At the same time, he finds it distressing that in order for him to eat meat, which he enjoys, forest animals must die: "And yet it irks me, the poor dappled fools . . . Should, in their own confines, with forked heads / Have their round haunches gor'd." Duke Senior expresses an exaggerated view of life in the country, which Jaques later enlarges upon.

When the First Lord recounts Jaques's sentimental grieving over the dying animal, Duke Senior is amused. He does not take Jaques's melancholy outbursts seriously. Jaques, on the other hand, believes his own words are profound. The two men also point out two often-debated views that were popular in that period: in nature everything is good (Duke Senior) and nature is good only if people are not around to change it (Jaques).

ACT II, SCENE 2

OVERVIEW

An irate Frederick discovers that Rosalind and Celia are missing from the palace, as is the court jester. "Can it be possible," he says, "that no man saw them?" A lord tells him that the gentlewoman to the princess overheard Rosalind and Celia speaking in praise of Orlando: "And she believes wherever they are gone / That youth is surely in their company." Frederick commands that if Orlando cannot be found, Oliver is to be brought before him. "I'll make him find him," says Frederick, who does not yet know of the falling-out between the brothers.

"THIS HOUSE IS BUT A BUTCHERY."

ANALYSIS

The anger and vengeance in this court scene contrasts with the quiet forest haven in the previous scene. Shakespeare often contrasted one scene to the previous for dramatic effect. Though the scene is brief, it also establishes cause for Oliver travel to the Forest of Arden later in the act.

ACT II, SCENE 3

OVERVIEW

When Orlando returns to Oliver's estate, Adam greets him with disturbing news. Oliver has learned of his victory over the wrestler. Since Charles did not harm Orlando, Oliver vows to do so. Orlando must leave immediately, says Adam: "This is no place; this house is but a butchery."

Orlando declares that he has no money and no way to make a living: "What, wouldst thou have me go and beg my food?" The old servant offers his savings to Orlando and asks to accompany the young man: "All this I give you. Let me be your servant." Orlando agrees and the two hurriedly leave for the Forest of Arden.

ANALYSIS

This scene sends the last two main characters from court life into the Forest of Arden to meet the rest of the players, who are the country folk. The goodness of faithful servant Adam—"Master, go on; and I will follow thee / To the last gasp, with truth and loyalty"—is contrasted here with the villainous acts of Oliver and Frederick.

ACT II, SCENE 4

OVERVIEW

Rosalind, disguised as Ganymede; Celia, dressed as a shepherdess; and Touchstone reach the Forest of Arden. As the weary trio pauses to rest, they are greeted by two shepherds, young Silvius and the elderly Corin. Silvius is wailing loudly about his love for Phebe, who apparently does not care for him:

> NO, CORIN, BEING OLD, THOU CANST NOT GUESS,
> THOUGH IN THY YOUTH THOU WAST AS TRUE A LOVER
> AS EVER SIGH'D UPON A MIDNIGHT PILLOW:
> BUT IF THY LOVE WERE EVER LIKE TO MINE
> AS SURE I THINK DID NEVER MAN LOVE SO
> HOW MANY ACTIONS MOST RIDICULOUS
> HAST THOU BEEN DRAWN TO BY THY FANTASY?

To which Corin replies, "Into a thousand that I have forgotten." The old shepherd tries to give advice but is ignored, and Silvius marches off.

Touchstone, who has been witnessing the conversation, makes witty fun of Silvius. Rosalind instead asks Corin for food and shelter. The shepherd says he has none to give: "I am shepherd to another man." He does, however, say that his master has a cottage and flock for sale. Silvius was supposed to buy them, but he is too distraught at the moment to worry about practical matters. Rosalind and Celia say they will give Corin the money to buy the cottage and flock, and will hire him as shepherd at a higher wage than he was earning.

ANALYSIS

In Silvius's distraught love for Phebe, Shakespeare introduces the concept that love can be foolish. Touchstone makes fun of foolish love, but in so doing he speaks two truths: "but as all is mortal in nature, so is all nature in love mortal in folly." He is saying that everything in the world is temporary, including the foolishness of love. Rosalind, too, is caught up in the foolishness of love, but unlike Silvius she is clever enough to recognize it as such.

Shakespeare also adds a bit of humor by including such a practical matter as buying a cottage and a flock of sheep into this otherwise implausible tale.

KURT RHODES, DIRECTOR OF THE HUDSON VALLEY SHAKESPEARE FESTIVAL 2007 PRODUCTION, SET AS YOU LIKE IT IN THE OLD WEST. JAQUES (CENTER, NANCE WILLIAMSON) SCOWLS AS TWO OF DUKE SENIOR'S MEN (RICARDO VAZQUEZ AND CLARK CARMICHAEL) SING.

ACT II, SCENE 5

OVERVIEW

Jaques, Amiens, and other lords stroll through the forest. Amiens begins to sing and some of the lords join him. Although Jaques urges more singing, he will not be drawn out of his melancholy. He has spent the day avoiding Duke Senior, who he says "is too disputable for my company." While Amiens sings along with Jaques's melancholy song, the others prepare a meal for the duke. Jaques decides to lie down and go to sleep, although in his state of mind he is not sure that sleep will come.

ANALYSIS

This scene deals with two primary points: city versus country setting and the character of Jaques. He is always ready to argue and always takes the opposing view, but he does not have the wisdom to make his observations meaningful. It is interesting that Jaques is the most antagonistic toward country life of all the characters in the play. Yet, at the end of the play, he will choose to remain in the forest.

ACT II, SCENE 6

OVERVIEW

Orlando and Adam finally reach the forest; both are tired and hungry. In fact, Adam says that he will soon die from lack of food: "Here lie I down and measure out my grave." Orlando comforts him and promises he will go ahead to find them food and shelter: "I will here be with thee presently, and if I bring thee not something to eat, I will give thee leave to die."

ANALYSIS

The scene is intentionally overdramatic as Adam declares he will soon die from lack of food. However, it also establishes Orlando, shown in his loyal treatment of Adam, as a youth of noble character. Gentle and good, he is always mindful of others and their needs. The scene finally puts Orlando in the Forest of Arden and also prepares for the young man's meeting with Duke Senior.

ACT II, SCENE 7

OVERVIEW

Duke Senior finally meets Jaques, who is uncharacteristically in good spirits. He recounts a meeting in the forest with a fool (Touchstone). Enchanted by Touchstone's witticisms, Jaques expresses the wish that he, too, could be a fool: "O that I were a fool! / I am ambitious for a motley coat." Duke Senior replies, "Thou shalt have one." A motley coat is the symbol of a fool, so the Duke is promising that Jaques shall have his wish.

Jaques says that as a fool he might be able "as the wind, / To blow on whom I please." He means that a fool can plainly speak his mind to expose the abuses in the world. Their conversation is eventually interrupted by Orlando, who enters with his sword drawn, intending to take food for himself and Adam.

The duke's kindness calms Orlando: "Sit down and feed, and welcome to our table." Accepting Duke Senior's offer, Orlando apologizes for his rude entrance: "Speak you so gently? Pardon me, I pray you: / I thought that all things had been savage here." (This is an indication of Orlando's ideas about rustic living.) Putting Adam's needs above his own, Orlando says he "will not touch a bit" of food until Adam "be first sufficed" and goes to get the old man.

"THOU SEE'ST WE ARE NOT ALL ALONE UNHAPPY."

While Orlando is fetching Adam, Jaques delivers one of Shakespeare's most well-known speeches. He opens saying, "All the world's a stage, / And all the men and women merely players." He means that everyone has a role to fill. From there, he goes on to describe the seven ages of man, beginning with the infant and ending with the senile, sick elder.

Orlando returns carrying Adam. They all sit down to eat. While Amiens sings "Blow, blow, thou winter wind," Orlando whispers his identity to Duke Senior, who welcomes "good Sir Roland's son" to the forest. After their meal they all retire to the duke's cave.

ANALYSIS

This scene shows Orlando's devotion to Adam, who is like a father to him. Orlando is willing to forgo food if it means that Adam will eat.

Also in this scene, it is obvious that Jaques is completely taken in by the wit of Touchstone. The court jester was being foolish on purpose, but Jaques believes Touchstone is so profound and wise that he wishes to be a clown, too.

Jaques's "All the world's a stage" speech is regarded by many critics as one of Shakespeare's most poetic and beautiful. The exchange between Jaques and Duke Senior also points out their basic differences. No matter what happens, Jaques is determined to be unhappy in this world. The duke, in contrast, is willing to make the best of whatever world he is in.

ACT III, SCENE 1

OVERVIEW

Back at court, Oliver reports to Frederick, saying he does not know his brother's whereabouts. Frederick replies that he had better return with Orlando within a year's time or he will lose his estate and possessions: "bring him dead or living / . . . or . . . / Thy lands, and all things that thou dost call thine / Worth seizure, do we seize into our hands."

Oliver protests that he never loved his brother. This fuels Frederick's anger and he says to Oliver, "More villain thou." Then he orders Oliver out of the palace.

ANALYSIS

Interestingly, Frederick says Oliver is a villain because he does not love his brother. But it seems Frederick is just as guilty for sending his own brother into exile. This scene also sends Oliver on his way to the Forest of Arden, where he will join the other characters.

ACT III, SCENE 2

OVERVIEW

Poor Orlando is so smitten that he wanders through the Forest of Arden hanging love poems on trees and carving Rosalind's name in the bark:

> HANG THERE, MY VERSE, IN WITNESS OF MY LOVE;
> AND THOU, THRICE-CROWNED QUEEN OF NIGHT, SURVEY
> WITH THY CHASTE EYE, FROM THY PALE SPHERE ABOVE,
> THY HUNTRESS' NAME THAT MY FULL LIFE DOTH SWAY.
> O ROSALIND ! THESE TREES SHALL BE MY BOOKS.

Touchstone and Corin begin a discussion of court versus country life. Corin contends that polite manners mean nothing in the country. Touchstone earnestly disagrees. Their conversation and Orlando's lovesickness are interrupted by disguised Rosalind. She is reading one of Orlando's poems that likens her to a jewel:

> FROM THE EAST TO WESTERN IND,
> NO JEWEL IS LIKE ROSALIND. . . .
> ALL THE PICTURES FAIREST LINED
> ARE BUT BLACK TO ROSALIND
> LET NO FACE BE KEPT IN MIND
> BUT THE FAIR OF ROSALIND.

Touchstone mocks the poem with his own nonsensical ditty in which he calls Rosalind too skinny and likens her to a nut:

> WINTER GARMENTS MUST BE LINED,
> SO MUST SLENDER ROSALIND.
> THEY THAT REAP MUST SHEAF AND BIND;
> THEN TO CART WITH ROSALIND.
> SWEETEST NUT HATH SOUREST RIND,
> SUCH A NUT IS ROSALIND.

Then he asks Rosalind why she bothers herself with such a "false gallop of verses." She replies: "Peace, you dull fool! I found them on a tree."

Now Celia enters, reading aloud another of Orlando's poems. She hints that she knows the author, and Rosalind begs her to reveal his name. Under Rosalind's barrage of questions, Celia reveals, "It is young Orlando, that tripped up the wrestler's heels and your heart both in an instant."

Soon after, Orlando and Jaques enter together. It is obvious that the two do not like each other. After some verbal sparring, mostly concerning Orlando's love for Rosalind, Jaques leaves. Rosalind, disguised as Ganymede, approaches Orlando. When she talks about the tree carvings, Orlando admits he is the culprit, hopelessly in love and beyond cure: "I swear to thee, youth, by the white hand of Rosalind, I am that he, that unfortunate he."

However, Rosalind, says she—rather, Ganymede—can cure him of this affliction. To do so, Orlando must go daily to the cottage of Ganymede and court the young man, who will pretend to be Rosalind. (Of course, Ganymede actually *is* Rosalind.) Ganymede claims to have cured another lovesick man this way:

> *HE WAS TO IMAGINE ME HIS LOVE, HIS MISTRESS;*
> *AND I SET HIM EVERY DAY TO WOO ME; AT WHICH*
> *TIME WOULD I, BEING BUT A MOONISH YOUTH,*
> *GRIEVE, BE EFFEMINATE, CHANGEABLE, LONG AND*
> *LIKING, PROUD, FANTASTICAL, APISH, SHALLOW,*
> *INCONSTANT, FULL OF TEARS, FULL OF SMILES, FOR*
> *EVERY PASSION SOMETHING AND FOR NO PASSION*
> *TRULY ANYTHING . . . . AND THUS I CURED HIM; AND*
> *THIS WAY WILL I TAKE UPON ME TO WASH YOUR*
> *LIVER AS CLEAN AS A SOUND SHEEP'S HEART, THAT*
> *THERE SHALL NOT BE ONE SPOT OF LOVE IN'T.*

Orlando agrees to be cured of lovesickness in this manner: "Now, by the faith of my love, I will."

ANALYSIS

Touchstone and Corin add more to the ongoing discussion of the merits of country and court living. Each finds the other's wit amusing. Once again, Shakespeare distinguishes the characters by using formal and informal language. Touchstone uses such familiar pronouns as "thou" when speaking to Corin and calls him "shepherd." Corin, on the other hand, addresses Touchstone as "you" or "master."

However, it is the arrangement for Rosalind to cure Orlando that provides even more amusement. Indeed this scene is one of the most humorous in the play. Rosalind reads Orlando's verses and even comments that they are not very good. However, she enjoys them because they are about her, so it really doesn't matter how bad they are. And as for Orlando, he is too much in love to care about how bad a poet he is. Since Rosalind is disguised as a young man, she can listen to Orlando's glowing description of her without his awareness of her identity. In Shakespeare's time, female roles were played by boys whose voices had not changed yet. So, an Elizabethan audience would be watching a boy playing a woman who is playing a man for the love of a man. This would have added another level of amusement to the production.

CELIA (MIRIAM SILVERMAN) LOOKS ON AS
DISGUISED ROSALIND (AMANDA QUAID)
READS ONE OF ORLANDO'S LOVE POEMS.

ACT III, SCENE 3

OVERVIEW

Not all the lovers in *As You Like It* are as romantic and compelling as Rosalind and Orlando. In another part of the forest, the witty Touchstone is wooing Audrey, who is perhaps Shakespeare's most dull-witted female character. Here is an exchange between them:

> AUDREY: WELL, I AM NOT FAIR; AND THEREFORE
> I PRAY THE GODS MAKE ME HONEST.
>
> TOUCHSTONE: TRULY, AND TO CAST AWAY
> HONESTY UPON A FOUL SLUT WERE TO PUT
> GOOD MEAT INTO AN UNCLEAN DISH.
>
> AUDREY: I AM NOT A SLUT, THOUGH
> I THANK THE GODS I AM FOUL.

Touchstone and Audrey are on their way to see the vicar, Sir Oliver Martext, to be married. But when they meet him, they realize they have no one to give the bride away. Jaques, who has been following the pair, says he will do so, though he admits to the audience that he does not support the union. However, he tells Touchstone that they should be married by a priest instead of the vicar: "And will you, being a man of your breeding, be married under a bush like a beggar?" If there is no priest to bless them, Jaques counsels, their marriage is not likely to last.

Touchstone, in an aside, says that he had hoped the vicar would marry him and Audrey precisely for this reason: "[the vicar] is not likely to marry me well; and not being well married, it will be a good excuse for me hereafter to leave my wife." He wants to consummate his relationship with Audrey and therefore arranges for Martext to marry them. Touchstone knows the vicar's incompetence would enable him to later abandon or cheat on Audrey without repercussion. However, by seeing through the jester's scheme, Jaques has forced Touchstone to find a priest to marry him and Audrey.

ANALYSIS

The romance between Touchstone and Audrey is amusing because it is so incongruous. Touchstone is a wily, city-wise man well versed in courtly ways, and Audrey is a dull-witted country bumpkin. Touchstone is trying to take advantage of Audrey by marrying her in a questionable ceremony that leaves him free to leave her once he is bored and his "desires" satisfied. The sexually motivated relationship contrasts Orlando and Rosalind's relationship, which is characterized by Orlando's flowery cavalier wooing and culminates in a union of equals with their marriage at the end of the play. Touchstone's willingness to use Audrey for his own pleasure, essentially treating her like an object, contrasts Silvius's idealization and adoration of Phebe.

In traditional pastoral literature, city dwellers travel to the forest to acquire wisdom from the country folk. Shakespeare uses the unintelligent Audrey to point out the foolishness of that notion. And a romance between the cerebral Touchstone and the clueless Audrey produces many laughs.

ACT III, SCENE 4

OVERVIEW

Rosalind is very upset because Orlando has not arrived at the cottage for his first session to cure his lovesickness. She tells Celia that she is about to weep because he is not there. Celia teases her at first, saying he is probably absent because, despite his lovesick actions and proclamations, he is really not in love: "but for his verity in love I do think him as concave as a covered goblet or a worm-eaten nut," both of which have exteriors that belie the empty insides. Then she adds that Orlando is with Rosalind's father, Duke Senior. Rosalind says that she actually met her father the day before and spoke to him. He did not recognize her in disguise; in fact, she says, "He asked me of what parentage I was." But Rosalind doesn't want to discuss her father "when there is such a man as Orlando" to think about.

Then Corin enters and tells the young women to come with him to watch Silvius trying to win the love of Phebe, a woman "of scorn and proud disdain" who does not return Silvius's love.

Rosalind's distress over Orlando's absence shows that she feels deeply for him. Celia, however, offers a much more rational—and even cynical—view of the budding relationship. She does not trust Orlando's intentions or sincerity. The juxtaposition of Rosalind's emotionality with Celia's practicality heightens the contrast between them.

Shakespeare cleverly follows the conversation between Rosalind and Celia with Corin's description of the unrequited "true love" Silvius has for Phebe. Whereas hearing about Silvius's devoted love delights Rosalind, who claims "the sight of lovers feedeth those in love," the situation also provides an example of what Celia fears: that Orlando doesn't reciprocate Rosalind's affections.

ACT III, SCENE 5

OVERVIEW

The disguised Rosalind and Celia have followed Corin, and the trio is eavesdropping on Phebe and Silvius. Silvius insists that Phebe will understand his feelings when she falls in love and Phebe responds, "Come not thou near me." Rosalind, unable to watch quietly any longer, interrupts the pair. She not-so-subtly tells Phebe that she should take what is offered (Silvius), because there won't be many other men interested in marrying her. Rosalind also scolds Silvius for flattering Phebe with his pursuit and feeding her vanity.

But instead of the desired effect, Phebe suddenly is attracted to Rosalind, or, rather, to Ganymede. Rosalind, Celia, and Corin leave. With Ganymede gone and only Silvius remaining, Phebe decides that since he speaks of love so eloquently, she will endure his company. However, she tells him, he should not expect more than that. Silvius asks just that she smile at him once in a while: "loose now and then / A scatter'd smile, and that I'll live upon." As they leave, Phebe says she will write Ganymede a taunting letter, to be delivered by Silvius, because he was so rude to her.

The confusion grows as Phebe now succumbs to love for Rosalind, who she thinks is a man. Elizabethan audiences delighted in this kind of gender switching. Rosalind tries to warn Phebe against falling in love with her male alter ego, for obvious reasons, saying: "I pray you, do not fall in love with me, / For I am falser than vows made in wine." She alludes to her disguise by admitting that she is "false."

ACT IV, SCENE 1

OVERVIEW

With Celia looking on, Rosalind (dressed as Ganymede) and Jaques have a discussion about his constant melancholy disposition. They have opposing viewpoints: Jaques thinks that it is good to be sad and say nothing, to which Rosalind replies that one might as well "be a post" because a post neither enjoys life nor speaks. Jaques says that reflecting on his experiences traveling, which left him with no land of his own, makes him sad. Rosalind replies: "I had rather have a fool to make me merry than experience to make me sad; and to travel for it too!"

Orlando finally arrives for his appointment with Ganymede, and Jaques leaves. Orlando, pretending Ganymede is Rosalind, asks for forgiveness. At first Rosalind chides him: "Why, how now, Orlando! Where have you been all this while? You a lover! An you serve me such another trick, never come in my sight more." She instructs Orlando to act as though she were Rosalind (which, of course, she is): "Come, woo me, woo me, for now I am in a holiday humour and like enough to consent. What would you say to me now, an I were your very very Rosalind?"

Orlando says, "I would kiss before I spoke," which Rosalind tells him is not a good idea. When she (as Ganymede) refuses Orlando's appeals, he dramatically declares that he will perish: "Then in mine own person I die." Rosalind smartly retorts that no one has ever died of love, so he won't either.

Rosalind and Orlando ask Celia to pretend to be a priest and marry them. After Orlando vows to take Rosalind as his wife, Rosalind explains that for women "the sky changes when they are wives." Rosalind claims that, because she is a woman, she will be jealous, fickle, emotional, and uncooperative once she is married. Orlando protests such a notion, but then remembers that he has a meeting with Duke Senior. He says he will return by two o'clock.

He leaves, and Celia scolds Rosalind for the disparaging things she has said about the female sex. Rosalind's defense is that she is quite out of her mind with love for Orlando.

She declares that she will "go find a shadow and sigh till he come." Rosalind is the epitome of the pining lover. The more practical Celia decides to go to sleep.

ANALYSIS

Witty Rosalind seems to enjoy her discourse with Jaques, but he remains largely unaware of her teasing. When she chides him about traveling to gain experience, she is actually making fun of many Englishmen of the time who traveled to the Continent (meaning the rest of Europe) and returned with affected speech and mannerisms.

There is much sweetness and humor in the banter with Orlando because Rosalind is so obviously delighted to be with him. She is as intensely in love as he, but she reacts differently. She does not go to the extremes that Orlando does: whereas he claims he'll die without her, she tells him that no one ever died of love. When Rosalind mocks the female sex, she is trying to convey that there is no such thing as the perfect woman, which Orlando seems to think Rosalind is. Actually, she wants both of them to be more realistic about what they feel for each other. She wants their relationship to survive anywhere—even outside the serene atmosphere of Arden.

Although Orlando is unaware of it because of the disguise, Rosalind is telling him what she will be like when they marry: "I will be more jealous of thee than a Barbary cock-pigeon over his hen . . . more giddy in my desires than a monkey." In other words, she will be no submissive lady. While dressed as Ganymede, Rosalind can use language that would be embarrassing for her to use as a woman.

ACT IV, SCENE 2

OVERVIEW

In this short scene, which is used to indicate the passage of time while the events to be described in scene 3 take place, one of Duke Senior's lords has killed a deer. Jaques sarcastically suggests that the lords should present the deer to the Duke "like a Roman conqueror" and asks if the lord knows an appropriate song. The lord obliges:

> WHAT SHALL HE HAVE THAT KILL'D THE DEER?
> HIS LEATHER SKIN AND HORNS TO WEAR,
> THEN SING HIM HOME;
> THE REST SHALL BEAR THIS BURDEN.
> TAKE THOU NO SCORN TO WEAR THE HORN;
> IT WAS A CREST ERE THOU WAST BORN;
> THY FATHER'S FATHER WORE IT,
> ANY THY FATHER BORE IT;
> THE HORN, THE HORN, THE LUSTY HORN
> IS NOT A THING TO LAUGH TO SCORN.

ANALYSIS

Once again, Jaques is the critic. The song that the lord sings makes reference to the horns of a deer. That is also a reference to a husband with an unfaithful wife, known as a cuckold. Elizabethan audiences always found that subject amusing.

ACT IV, SCENE 3

OVERVIEW

Now past two o'clock, it is Silvius who arrives at the cottage, not Orlando. Silvius carries the letter to Ganymede written by Phebe. He says she was angry when she wrote it. Rosalind at first says the letter is "cruel" and "railing," but as she reads it aloud, both she and Silvius realize that Phebe has written a poem of love. Rosalind sends the shepherd back to tell Phebe that unless she loves Silvius, Ganymede could never love Phebe.

The next arrival is a surprise; it is Oliver looking for Ganymede. He hands Rosalind a bloody handkerchief. Oliver explains that he was searching for Orlando in the forest and fell asleep under an oak tree. While he was sleeping, a snake coiled around his neck. When Orlando approached the snake was frightened away, but that caused a nearby hungry lioness to awaken. Before the lioness pounced on the sleeping Oliver, Orlando momentarily debated whether he should let his wicked brother die. But he killed the lioness and saved Oliver's life. Oliver was so overwhelmed by his brother's brave deed that his hatred changed to love.

After the attack, the two brothers returned to Duke Senior's cave. There, Orlando discovered that he had a gash in his arm from the lioness. He bandaged it with the handkerchief that Oliver now presents to Rosalind. She promptly faints. That causes Oliver to say, "You lack a man's heart," which, of course, she does. Rosalind protests rather weakly that the fainting was only an act. Ganymede fainted because that is what the fair Rosalind, Orlando's love, would have done.

Rosalind is not sure if Silvius is aware of the contents of Phebe's letter, which is why she only pretends to read it at first. When she realizes it is a love poem, she tries—unsuccessfully—to hide its meaning from Silvius. Although Celia expresses pity for Silvius, calling him a poor shepherd, Rosalind, playing the manly Ganymede, says he deserves no pity because love has turned him into a tame snake.

Modern audiences might find it difficult to believe Oliver's sudden change of heart toward his brother. But in plays from Elizabethan times, sudden conversions were acceptable and commonplace. Shakespeare has similar changes occur in some of his other plays, such as Bertram's sudden switch from hate to love for Helena in *All's Well That Ends Well.*

Another important thing to note, once again, is the characteristics of male and female behavior that were so important in Shakespeare's time. Rosalind dresses like a man and acts like a man. But when she is confronted with frightening news such as Orlando's fight with the lioness, she faints, an action considered quintessentially female in Shakespeare's time.

This scene also moves the play toward resolution. Some critics suggest that Orlando must have some idea of Ganymede's true identity by this point in the play. Furthermore, the closer they get to romance, the more certain her disguise will be discovered.

ACT V, SCENE 1

OVERVIEW

As they walk through the forest, Audrey whines to Touchstone that she is impatient for the marriage. She says that the vicar would have been "good enough" to marry them. But Touchstone calls Sir Oliver, the vicar, "a most vile Martext." Then he speaks of a youth in the forest who fancies Audrey. William appears on cue and Touchstone asks if he is wise. William replies,

TOUCHSTONE (STEPHEN PAUL JOHNSON) TALKS TO AN ADORING AUDREY (PAUL BATES). DIRECTOR KURT RHODES PLAYED UP THE COMEDY IN HIS 2007 STAGING BY CASTING A MAN AS THE DIM-WITTED SHEPHERDESS.

"Ay, sir, I have a pretty wit." That is all Touchstone has to hear as he reduces the young rustic to silence with his fancy words. In no uncertain terms, Touchstone lets William know that Audrey is not available: "Therefore, you clown, abandon,—which is in the vulgar leave,—the society,—which in the boorish is company,—of this female."

William meekly leaves and Corin enters. He says that Ganymede and Aliena want to see Touchstone. The three of them leave.

ANALYSIS

William, like the other country characters, is used by Shakespeare to contrast city and country living. As opposed to Touchstone's verbose sophistication, William answers in sentences of only a few words. However, Touchstone goes so overboard in his tirade—such as "I will kill thee a hundred and fifty ways; therefore tremble, and depart"—that he ends up seeming foolish to the audience.

ACT V, SCENE 2

OVERVIEW

Oliver has apparently fallen in love with Aliena (unaware that she is really Ferdinand's daughter Celia), but Orlando is skeptical. "Is't possible that on so little acquaintance you should like her?" he asks Oliver, despite the fact that Orlando also fell in love at first sight. Oliver is so in love that he wants to become a shepherd to marry Aliena and pledges to give Orlando "all the revenue that was old Sir Roland's," effectively reversing the situation that caused the falling out between the two brothers at the beginning of the play. With Orlando's approval, the wedding is set for the next day.

Rosalind, still disguised as Ganymede, arrives, and Orlando admits that the thought of his brother's marriage fills him with sadness because he is without his own love. Considering the circumstances, Rosalind cleverly tells Orlando that she is a "magician." She promises that when Oliver marries his love the next day, Orlando will marry Rosalind.

Silvius and Phebe arrive. Silvius talks about loving Phebe, Phebe talks about loving Ganymede, and Orlando pines for Rosalind. Rosalind tells them all to be quiet: "no more of this; 'tis like the howling of Irish wolves against the moon." She assures them they will all be married the next day.

To Silvius she says: "I will help you, if I can." To Phebe, she says: "I would love you, if I could." To Orlando, she says: "I will satisfy you, if ever I satisfied man, and you shall be married tomorrow." The group departs.

ANALYSIS

Once again, one of the characters has suddenly and insanely fallen in love, in this case Oliver with the disguised Celia. Back at court, Oliver would never have loved a common shepherdess, but in the forest the insanity of love is master. This romance also pushes Rosalind into a decision. She can no longer watch Orlando's distress over the thought that his brother will marry, but not he. The audience realizes that the disguise is just about over. Ganymede will have to undress, so to speak.

The romantic extremes of Oliver, Silvius, and Phebe also highlight the equally intense but more sophisticated feelings of Rosalind and Orlando. At least they have engaged in some conversation before giving themselves over to romantic love.

Rosalind notes that she is capable of magic, a matter of much interest to Elizabethan audiences. During this period, ignorance and fear of the unknown resulted in many superstitions. People believed in magic and mystical properties of animals and herbs. Rosalind's suggestion also foreshadows the appearance of Hymen, the god of marriage, in the last scene.

ACT V, SCENE 3

OVERVIEW

"To-morrow will we be married," says Touchstone to Audrey. To emphasize the occasion, two of Duke Senior's pages appear and sing a song about a lover and his lass. It compares love to springtime and includes such nonsense lines as, "With a hey, and a ho, and hey nonino." Touchstone ridicules the performance: "By my troth, yes; I count it but time lost to hear such a foolish song. God be wi' you; and God mend your voices!"

This short scene prepares the audience for the elaborate spectacle on the next day. Touchstone may be correct in ridiculing the notion that love is like springtime or that birds sing "ding a ding, ding" for lovers. However, the attraction between Touchstone and Audrey is first and foremost physical. As such, he misses out on the sheer beauty of just being in love. As for simple Audrey, at least here she does reflect a bit on marriage to Touchstone: "I do desire it with all my heart; and I hope it is no dishonest desire to desire to be a woman of the world."

ACT V, SCENE 4

OVERVIEW

The wedding day has arrived. Three couples—Rosalind (still in disguise) and Orlando, Celia (still in disguise) and Oliver, and Phebe and Silvius—are gathered along with Duke Senior and Jaques. Rosalind uses her alter ego, Ganymede, to get them all to agree to certain terms: Orlando will marry Rosalind if she shows up, and Phebe will marry Ganymede unless she refuses for some reason, in which case she will marry Silvius. All parties agree.

Rosalind and Celia leave, and Duke Senior muses that Ganymede resembles his own daughter. Orlando agrees: "My lord, the first time that I ever saw him, / Me thought he was a brother to your daughter."

Touchstone and Audrey arrive. Jaques introduces Touchstone as a supposed "courtier." The jester says that he has danced, flattered women, schemed, ordered lots of clothes from tailors, and quarreled to prove that he is familiar with courtly life. At Jaques's prodding, Touchstone recounts how one quarrel almost led to a duel.

But suddenly all that is interrupted by the soft strains of music. Hymen, the god of marriage, has arrived. He is accompanied by Rosalind and

Celia, who are now dressed as themselves. Orlando says, "If there be truth in sight, you are my Rosalind." All parties agree to keep their promises. Orlando will marry Rosalind. Oliver will marry Celia. Phebe agrees to marry Silvius. And so, with the addition of Touchstone and Audrey, the couples are married.

Now enters Jaques du Boys, brother of Oliver and Orlando, with another surprise. Frederick came to the forest to seek out his brother, Duke Senior, and destroy him. Instead he encountered an old religious man:

> AND TO THE SKIRTS OF THIS WILD WOOD HE CAME;
> WHERE MEETING WITH AN OLD RELIGIOUS MAN,
> AFTER SOME QUESTION WITH HIM, WAS CONVERTED
> BOTH FROM HIS ENTERPRISE AND FROM THE WORLD,
> HIS CROWN BEQUEATHING TO HIS BANISH'D BROTHER,
> AND ALL THEIR LANDS RESTORED TO THEM AGAIN
> THAT WERE WITH HIM EXILED. THIS TO BE TRUE,
> I DO ENGAGE MY LIFE.

It seems that this encounter caused Frederick to convert. He has decided to retreat from the world and to leave his throne and all his lands once again to his brother. Duke Senior is elated: "Play music! And you, brides and bridegrooms all, / With measure heap'd in joy, to the measures fall."

Now everyone can return to court. Duke Senior asks melancholy Jaques to stay for the wedding feast, but he declines. He will join Frederick and the religious converts: "To see no pastime I; what you would have / I'll stay to know at your abandon'd cave." He gives appropriate goodbyes to each:

To Duke Senior: "You to your former honour I bequeath."

To Orlando: "You to a love that your true faith doth merit."

To Oliver: "You to your land and love and great allies."

To Silvius: "You to a long and well-deserved bed."

To Touchstone: "And you to wrangling; for thy loving voyage / Is but for two months victuall'd."

With that, the melancholy, but in this case well-spoken, Jaques leaves as the happy couples prepare for the wedding dance. So concludes the merry romp that is *As You Like It*.

ANALYSIS

Interestingly enough, Shakespeare reverses the lives of the main characters in the end. Duke Senior and the others have spent the play extolling the pleasures of country living, but now they will return to the court. Jaques, who has criticized everything about the country, will spend his life there. He remains, from beginning to end, a man apart.

This reversal should not be read as the virtue of one lifestyle over the other. Rather, there are merits in both, as exhibited by the characters that cross this boundary.

Rosalind makes good on her promise to straighten out all problems among the lovers. It is quite probable, judging from the conversation between Duke Senior and Orlando, that her true identity was discovered before she revealed it. However that does not detract from her charade. It forms a good deal of the charming spell between the two main lovers.

EPILOGUE

OVERVIEW

Alone on stage, Rosalind admits that it is unusual for a woman to deliver the epilogue, but promises to bewitch the audience. She asks of the women to like as much of the play as they want to. Of the men she says that "If I were a woman, I would kiss as many of you as had beards that pleased me, complexions that liked me, and breaths that I defied not." The humor here for the Elizabethan audience was that the role of Rosalind was always played by a young and beardless boy. She exits by saying that, after her curtsy, the audience would produce a nice round of applause:

AND, I AM SURE, AS MANY AS HAVE GOOD BEARDS OR GOOD FACES OR SWEET BREATHS WILL, FOR MY KIND OFFER, WHEN I MAKE CURTSY, BID ME FAREWELL.

With that short epilogue the curtain closes. The main characters will leave the forest and return to a life at court.

ANALYSIS

To enter the Forest of Arden is to have a merry romp with the parade of characters, countrified or of the court. The rules of society are suspended, enabling romance to blossom. The characters delight in teasing and mystifying each other, and that goes for the audience as well.

ROSALIND (LIA WILLIAMS), IN DISGUISE AS GANYMEDE, AND ORLANDO (BARNABY KAY) HAVE AN AWKWARD MOMENT WHILE READING ONE OF ORLANDO'S LOVE POEMS.

LIST OF CHARACTERS

Rosalind: Clever, independent-minded daughter of Duke Senior who falls in love with Orlando; she is a fitting heroine

Orlando de Boys: Youngest son of deceased Sir Roland and the play's hero; a noble young man who has been wronged by his brother

Oliver de Boys: Older, begrudging brother of Orlando who denies him a gentleman's education

Duke Senior: Rosalind's father, and rightful ruler of the dukedom, who is banished to the Forest of Arden

Frederick: Duke Senior's villainous brother and usurper of the throne

Celia: Frederick's daughter, as well as cousin and dearest friend to Rosalind

Touchstone: Witty court jester who accompanies Rosalind and Celia to the Forest of Arden

Adam: Elderly, loyal de Boys servant who accompanies Orlando to the Forest of Arden

Charles: Professional wrestler whom Oliver pits against Orlando

Jaques: Melancholy follower of Duke Senior who regards himself as a man of the world

Silvius: Young shepherd in love with Phebe

Phebe: Shepherdess who disdains Silvius's affections; she falls for Ganymede, who is Rosalind in disguise

Corin: Old shepherd who tries to teach Silvius about love

Audrey: Simple young country girl who does not understand Touchstone but loves him

William: Country boy who loves Audrey

Amiens: Song-loving lord who attends to Duke Senior in the Forest of Arden

Dennis: Servant to Oliver

Le Beau: Gentleman in Frederick's court

Sir Oliver Martext: A vicar

Jaques de Boys: Brother of Orlando and Oliver who is better treated by Oliver

Hymen: God of marriage

ANALYSIS OF MAJOR CHARACTERS

ROSALIND

Witty, warm, and intelligent, Rosalind has all the best virtues of the ideal Renaissance woman. She is the dominant character in the play, outshining even Orlando with her strength and integrity. She is strong-willed and independent, but able to laugh at herself and her emotional feelings. Although she is critical of others, she is no less critical of herself.

Rosalind is also a good judge of character. She sees through the worldly pretensions of Jaques. She grasps the occasional foolishness of Touchstone. She scolds Phebe for not accepting Silvius's love. She chides herself for her emotional reaction when Orlando is late for their meeting.

When Rosalind is exiled from court, she takes charge of her future. Instead of running off in tears, she decides to disguise herself as a male, which will give her more freedom and boldness. Remember that in Elizabethan times freedom for women was quite limited. Rosalind uses this pretense to show Orlando how to become a more gentle and skillful lover. Disguised as a male, she can talk to Orlando "man to man" and give

I WOULD KISS BEFORE I SPOKE.

him advice he would not accept from a woman. Yet her male disguise does not overtake her true emotions: she frets when Orlando is late for their appointment and faints upon hearing of Orlando's wound.

Rosalind is the central figure for all the lovers in this play. She is the only one who understands the difference between love as it really is and love as one might want it to be. She tells Silvius and Phebe that they have unrealistic ideas of what love should be and therefore cannot experience real joy. She tells Phebe to be realistic about the world in which she lives and to stop trying to live in the world she has imagined:

> FOR I MUST TELL YOU FRIENDLY IN YOUR EAR,
> SELL WHEN YOU CAN: YOU ARE NOT FOR ALL MARKETS;
> CRY THE MAN MERCY; LOVE HIM; TAKE HIS OFFER;
> FOUL IS MOST FOUL, BEING FOUL TO BE A SCOFFER,
> SO TAKE HER TO THEE, SHEPHERD: FARE YOU WELL. (III.5)

Rosalind wants to discuss love in a way that will keep her anchored in real life. To be false about love is to miss its true joy and beauty.

The one criticism audiences might have of Rosalind is her apparent lack of feeling for her father, Duke Senior. At first she is depressed about his exile, but she does not choose to join him. Even when she herself is exiled, she does not hurry off to meet him and does not express any desire to see him. However, her actions might be explained by the fact that by this time she is hopelessly in love with Orlando and can think of no one else. There is great charm to the character of Rosalind, whether she is bantering with Jaques or Touchstone or gently teasing Orlando about his skills as a lover.

ORLANDO

Orlando is a refreshing exception to many of Shakespeare's heroes. He is of noble character, kind, and thoughtful, and he is lively both in thought and action. For instance, in *Romeo and Juliet*, Romeo also acts in a lively manner. In his thoughts, however, he is very serious, especially for a teenager. Orlando does not spend his time thinking of consequences: he instantly rebels against his brother's treatment of him; he boldly challenges the wrestler even though he knows what Charles has done to opponents; he takes off for the Forest of Arden with hardly a moment's thought once he learns his brother is planning to harm him. And once he is caught in the throes of love, Orlando is both spontaneous and frivolous, attaching love poems to trees. In short, he is a most likeable character.

Orlando is able to profit from the instructions of Rosalind in her disguise. He does not mind acknowledging the fact that his poetry is very bad. He loves his feelings more than his words.

Interestingly, for all Orlando's virtues, he comes off as a bit less bright than Rosalind. That is as Shakespeare intended, for the character of Rosalind does dominate this play. Orlando might not possess her insight, but his generous spirit and his bravery are evident. In fact, Orlando is an ideal Elizabethan hero—courteous, gentle, strong, independent, and possessed of a nimble wit. He is also the ideal Elizabethan lover, a physically strong hero who is not afraid to surrender to lunacy when he meets his own true love. Never once does Orlando waver in his feelings for Rosalind, even though he has no idea when he will see her again. Since the play was first performed, audiences have adored Orlando.

THERE IS NO TRUTH IN HIM.

From the first act on, Orlando laments his lack of education that would turn him into a gentleman. Yet time and again throughout the play, his actions indicate that he is indeed a gentleman. He cares for Adam. He saves his brother's life. He exhibits unashamed affection for Rosalind. It would seem that the young man who says he lacks a gentleman's education acts more like a gentleman than those, such as Oliver, Frederick, and Jaques, who have received a proper education.

JAQUES

For Jaques, all the world is indeed a stage, and he is comfortable with playing the role of the melancholy gentleman. He laments everything, from the death of a deer to the fate of humans as they go through the seven ages of man. He is interested in what is happening in the world around him only as it relates to himself. Shakespeare makes it clear early in the play that there is nothing more to know about Jaques. He criticizes just for the sake of criticism. Rosalind, in contrast, is critical of Orlando because she wants him to become a more thoughtful lover.

Jaques has a biting sense of humor. When one of the lords sings a tune, Jaques adds the nonsense word *ducdame*. When asked what it means, he says it is an invocation calling fools into a circle. That might describe the lords themselves.

Jaques also feels a kinship with Touchstone, whom he regards as witty and brilliant. Jaques believes himself to be as witty as Touchstone, but, in fact, throughout the play Jaques truly does not grasp the jester's meaning at all. Though they both reject the ideal, Touchstone does so because he is a realist, while Jaques does so because he is a disappointed idealist.

Both Rosalind and Orlando instantly dislike Jaques, and he returns the sentiment. Rosalind dislikes Jaques because he is a malcontent and cannot find reason for merriment and, therefore, does not understand it in others.

MELANCHOLY JAQUES (JOSEPH MARCELL) IS TOO INSIGHTFUL AND DEEP FOR AMIENS (JON REYNOLDS) AND A COURTIER (MATTHEW MCGLOIN), WHO BOTH LISTEN WITH PUZZLED EXPRESSIONS IN THE 2007 FOLGER THEATRE PRODUCTION.

Jaques has already made up his mind that life is a sad affair, and he will spend no time trying to learn otherwise. In contrast, Rosalind wants the full value of her feelings for Orlando even if that invites the risk of loss. Orlando dislikes Jaques because his constant melancholy outlook clashes with Orlando's zest for life and love. Jaques's pessimism annoys Rosalind and Orlando, who are both optimists.

In his ever-penetrating melancholy, he forms a good contrast to the romantic capers of the four couples who are the love stories in the play. It is appropriate that Jaques is the one who will not return to court at the end of the play. Let the others rejoice in happiness and the insanity of love; melancholy Jaques will stay behind in the serenity of the forest.

TOUCHSTONE

Many of Shakespeare's plays incorporate a court jester or clown, but in Touchstone he has created one of the most witty, most gentle, and most happy. Touchstone is out of his element for most of the play. He is far more sophisticated in his wit and humor than the country folk with whom he interacts. He feels superior to them in intellect and worldliness, and he is. He observes what is going on around him and, with his commentary, he contributes to the audience's understanding of what is happening in the play. Most times, his observations are received with good humor by the other characters. When he makes fun of Orlando's bad poetry, Rosalind laughs, too. When he criticizes Corin for the pastoral life, it is taken as good-natured jesting. Yet at times Touchstone gets carried away with himself and his witticisms, to the extent that he comes off as a fool, because his comments are so exaggerated.

Touchstone may offer humor in his comments, but he is also the object of much humor himself in his feelings for Audrey, a dull-witted country lass. He makes no secret of the fact that lust is the basis of his attraction to her. He never tries to deceive anyone about his intentions concerning Audrey. Touchstone is fully aware that lust is not the best basis for a lasting marriage, and it is somewhat surprising that Touchstone would agree to be married at all. However, for him, happiness comes from physical pleasure, which he is not guaranteed unless he weds Audrey, and from having a quick wit. It seems an unlikely marriage, but Shakespeare makes it another expression of the folly that is love.

CELIA

Throughout the play, Celia fulfills a supporting role to Rosalind. The two girls are much alike in background, intelligence, humor, and physical attractiveness. Celia, too, embodies many of the qualities of the ideal heroine of the period. But her biggest role in this comedy is as a mirror to Rosalind, which makes Rosalind's qualities all the more obvious to the audience. Celia's practicality contrasts Rosalind's emotional tendencies.

The affection shared by the two young women is an important part of the play. Celia comforts her cousin when Rosalind is banished from court, and even suggests that the two of them will go into exile together. She gives up the richness and ease of court life to be with her dearest friend.

In most public conversations, Celia appears reserved, although she possesses great wit and charm as evidenced by her conversations with Rosalind. Throughout the play, she is not in love with or interested in anyone and is therefore able to maintain a rational mindset that contrasts—and emphasizes—Rosalind's lovesick swoons. It comes almost as a surprise, then, that she suddenly falls for the changed and appealing Oliver.

THE FOOL DOTH THINK HE IS WISE.

A CLOSER LOOK

- THEMES

- MOTIFS

- SYMBOLS

- LANGUAGE

- INTERPRETING THE PLAY

The British Shakespeare ▶
Company performed *As You
Like It* as part of the 2007
Leeds Shakespeare Festival.

British
Shakespeare
Company

LEEDS
SHAKESPEARE
FESTIVAL
24TH JULY TO 18TH AUGUST 2007

"Britain's largest and
best loved open air
Shakespeare company"
THE BBC

As You
Like
it

STARRING
STACEY ROCA
(BBC THE OFFICE)
AND
JAMES
ALEXANDROU

OPEN-AIR THEATRE AT KIRKSTALL ABBEY

Tickets from £15 to £25 Concessions £3 off
City Centre Box Office **0113 224 3801** Gateway Yorkshire **0113 242 5242**
24 hour ticket hotline **0870 040 00**
www.britishshakespearecompany

66929 **Chapter Three** 66929

CHAPTER
THREE

a Closer Look

THEMES

CITY LIFE VERSUS COUNTRY LIFE

As a pastoral comedy, *As You Like It* thrives on the theme of city, or court, life versus country life. The play opens with depictions of the courtly lifestyle as being plagued by malevolence and injustice: Orlando is mistreated by his brother Oliver, and Duke Senior and Rosalind are banished by Frederick.

The setting then moves to the Forest of Arden, which is depicted as a calm, restful, and healing atmosphere. At first Arden seems a place of never-ending charm. Charles the wrestler describes Duke Senior's life in the forest in Act I, Scene 1: "They say many young gentlemen flock to him every day, and fleet the time carelessly, as they did in the golden world."

But in Act II, Scene 1, Duke Senior talks of his new surroundings more realistically: "Are not these woods / More free from peril than the envious court?" He continues, "And this our life exempt from public haunt / Finds tongues in trees, books in the running brooks, / Sermons in stones and good in every thing." The duke accepts the fact that there is adversity even in the forest. The weather is often brutal, obtaining food can be a problem, and dangerous animals are not far away. However, under the circumstances, Duke Senior concludes that he would not change his lifestyle.

The jester Touchstone is less enthusiastic about life in the country. When he arrives from court with Rosalind and Celia, he concludes, "Ay, now am I in Arden; the more fool I; when I was at home, I was in a better place; but travelers must be content" (II.4). He calls himself foolish for leaving the comforts of court for a rustic life. Later, when Corin asks how Touchstone likes the shepherd's life, the jester amusingly replies:

> . . . IN RESPECT OF ITSELF, IT IS A GOOD LIFE; BUT IN RESPECT THAT IT IS A SHEPHERD'S LIFE, IT IS NAUGHT. IN RESPECT THAT IT IS SOLITARY, I LIKE IT VERY WELL, BUT IN RESPECT THAT IT IS PRIVATE, IT IS A VERY VILE LIFE. NOW, IN RESPECT IT IS IN THE FIELDS, IT PLEASETH ME WELL; BUT IN RESPECT IT IS NOT IN COURT, IT IS TEDIOUS. (III.2)

As for melancholy Jaques, he never sees much good in anything. He believes that men and women should not even be in the forest since it rightly belongs to the animals.

Interestingly, Duke Senior and his lords, while extolling the restful benefits of life in Arden, continue to act much as they would at court. Rather than adapting to the forest, they make the forest adapt to them. Instead of doing physical work, they hold philosophical discussions at every opportunity. And even as they praise the shepherd's life, none of them would ever consider raising sheep or tending to the gardens. (For that matter, the supposed sheepherders Corin and Audrey never spend time caring for sheep either.) Indeed, the exiled players act precisely as if they were at court, minus the intrigues and bustle of that life. And at the end, with the exception of Frederick and Jaques, they all return to the city just about the same as when they left it.

In essence, Shakespeare is saying that there is good and bad in both country and city living. One does not outweigh the other. There is a necessary balance between the two. Duke Senior and his followers benefit from the therapeutic serenity of the forest. They are free to talk openly under the trees. They are free from the deceits of court. They are free to roam as they wish. However, in the end, they willingly return to court because it offers the style and sophistication that they crave. Thus, the restoration of one's mental balance in the country allows a person to return to the city more capable of dealing with urban life. With this new sense of balance, lovers will be more aware of their true feelings. Brothers will have a better understanding of each other. Both city and country living are important to the human experience.

THE NATURE OF LOVE

By Shakespeare's time, traditions were long established concerning the nature of love. To be in love is to be in torment. Love is a disease. It is painful. It is agony. It causes such great suffering to the lover that it reduces him or her to the role of slave to the beloved. It also tends to turn the lover into a scatterbrain. Why would anyone want to fall in love under these circumstances? Shakespeare shows in *As You Like It* that people don't have a choice when it comes to falling in love. He also plays with the idea of love as both pleasure and pain. Those characters who rejoice in their own suffering for love are often ridiculed and may even laugh at themselves.

Love affects four different couples in this play in different ways. The action moves back and forth among them, allowing the audience to

A LOVESICK SILVIUS (MICHAEL BORRELLI) PROFESSES HIS LOVE FOR PHEBE (VALERI MUDEK), SURROUNDED BY HER FLOCK.

compare the relationships. The audience also sees how the characters in love each react to his or her situation, and how outside characters react to each relationship.

First and foremost, there is Rosalind and Orlando, perhaps Shakespeare's happiest couple. Instantly taken with each other, they fall deeply in love but react in different ways. When Orlando first meets Rosalind in Act I, Scene 2, after he has defeated Charles in a wrestling match, he is so overcome with emotion that he is speechless:

Poor Orlando's torment has only begun. By Act III, Scene 2, he is reduced to hanging sappy love poems on trees and carving Rosalind's name into their trunks. He has become her slave: "Heaven would that she these gifts should have, / And I to live and die her slave." His torment worsens. By Act IV, Scene 1, he is convinced that if he cannot have his beloved, death is the only answer for him. When Rosalind, disguised as Ganymede, asks what he will do if his beloved rejects him, Orlando replies, "Then in mine own person I die."

Rosalind is as deeply in love as Orlando. But what makes her one of Shakespeare's most delightful heroines is her ability to laugh at herself and to look at love realistically. She knows love is making her silly even as she revels in the feeling. Rosalind will not let her passion for Orlando, or his for her, be anything other than real. She understands that these giddy feelings between her and her beloved will not last. She wants the excitement of new love to grow into something real and lasting. It is for those reasons that, in the disguise of Ganymede, she instructs Orlando to shed the nonsense and enjoy the real emotion that is true love. She points out that no one actually dies of love:

THE POOR WORLD IS ALMOST SIX THOUSAND YEARS OLD, AND IN ALL THIS TIME THERE WAS NOT ANY MAN DIED IN HIS OWN PERSON . . . IN A LOVE-CAUSE. TROILUS HAD HIS BRAINS DASHED OUT WITH A GRECIAN CLUB; YET HE DID WHAT HE COULD TO DIE BEFORE, AND HE IS ONE OF THE PATTERNS OF LOVE. LEANDER, HE WOULD HAVE LIVED MANY A FAIR YEAR, THOUGH HERO HAD TURNED NUN, IF IT HAD NOT BEEN FOR A HOT MIDSUMMER NIGHT . . . BUT THESE ARE ALL LIES: MEN HAVE DIED FROM TIME TO TIME AND WORMS HAVE EATEN THEM, BUT NOT FOR LOVE. (IV.1)

It is interesting that when Rosalind speaks of love throughout the play, she does so in prose rather than more flowery poetic lines. She will not stray from the reality of the experience of love. It is wonderful, it is moving, it is delightful torment, but it is also real. She wants love to survive not in imagination but in the real world.

For Touchstone, the witty, gentle, and happy court jester, love is quite a different experience. He has no illusions about romantic love or, for that matter, about the rather dull-witted and slatternly Audrey, who will be his bride. He introduces her to Duke Senior in Act V, Scene 4, as "a poor virgin, sir, an ill-favoured thing, sir, but mine own."

Like Rosalind, Touchstone does not deceive himself when it comes to love. However, while Rosalind confronts the fact that new love must mellow and change, Touchstone avoids succumbing to romantic delusions. He is physically attracted to Audrey, and that is why he will marry her. As he says in Act III, Scene 3: "As the ox hath his bow, sir, the horse his curb and the falcon her bells, so man hath his desire; and as pigeons bill, so wedlock would be nibbling."

Touchstone is practical; the niceties of romantic nonsense are not for him. However, there is a hint of slightly more than sexual gratification in the jester's relationship, even if it is only a sense of ownership. In Act V, Scene 1, the country fellow William admits that he is fond of Audrey. Touchstone's reaction is to insult the poor lad in an onslaught of words, calling him a clown and claiming that he will be killed in "a hundred and fifty ways." Shortly thereafter, Touchstone introduces his Audrey to Duke Senior and then marries her.

Then there is the seemingly rocky relationship between the smitten and untutored shepherd Silvius and the disdainful Phebe. Silvius is indeed the tortured lover. In Act III, Scene 5, he asks that Phebe at least notice his pain: "If ever – as that ever may be near, – / You meet in some fresh cheek the power of fancy, / Then shall you know the wounds invisible / That love's keen arrows make." By asking for her attention, Silvius is implying that his love pains can be cured by her. He wallows in self-indulgent misery. The scornful Phebe, however, remains unmoved and even adds insult to injury by expressing an interest in Ganymede, the disguised Rosalind. In the end, Silvius and Phebe are married. However, the marriage takes place because Rosalind makes Phebe promise that if she cannot have Ganymede (which, of course, she cannot because Ganymede is Rosalind), then she will marry Silvius. On this less-than-romantic footing, the wedding takes place.

Also of questionable romantic foundation is the union between Oliver, former villain, and Celia. In Act IV, Scene 3, after being saved by Orlando, Oliver repents his evil ways and becomes a good brother. This sudden transformation seems odd to modern readers, but was an oft-used device in Elizabethan plays. Oliver undergoes a second, equally sudden change when he falls in love with Celia, who is disguised as Aliena. Celia is immediately in love with Oliver but, unlike Rosalind, does not take part in her own courtship.

In *As You Like It*, not all marriages are made in heaven, and not all love is romantic and ideal. Perhaps Shakespeare is saying that in matters of love, nothing is quite as we like it.

STAGES OF HUMAN EXPERIENCE

Jaques is a moody cynic who cannot find reason or cause to be happy. He is forever expounding the generally unsatisfying state of the world—his own pessimistic view of it, at least. For all that, in Act II, Scene 7, Jaques delivers one of Shakespeare's most famous monologues, known as the Seven Ages of Man, which was a popular concept in Elizabethan England.

First he sets the background: "All the world's a stage, / And all the men and women merely players: / They have their exits and their entrances; / And one man in his time plays many parts, / His acts being seven ages."

IAN BANNEN AND VANESSA REDGRAVE
PLAYED LOVERS ORLANDO
AND ROSALIND IN A 1962 STAGE
PRODUCTION OF *AS YOU LIKE IT.*

Jaques then explains each age of man.

First Age: "At first the infant, / Mewling and puking in the nurse's arms." Logically, Jaques starts with infancy. Jaques emphasizes the crying and spitting up, suggesting that unhappiness is already present in this first age of life.

Second Age: "And then the whining school-boy, with his satchel / And shining morning face, creeping like snail, / Unwillingly to school." Instead of focusing on childhood games, Jaques defines this age with an image of a young boy begrudgingly going to school. He is forced to do something that makes him unhappy.

Third Age: "And then the lover, / Sighing like furnace, with a woeful ballad, / Made to his mistress' eyebrow." Jaques highlights the frustrations, not the pleasures, in love experienced by a young man in the third age.

Fourth Age: "Then a soldier, / Full of strange oaths and bearded like the pard, / Jealous in honour, sudden and quick in quarrel, / Seeking the bubble reputation / Even in the cannon's mouth." Age four is adulthood. Man is full of energy and seeks to make a name for himself, but he notes how this often results in dangerous, volatile situations.

Fifth Age: "And then the justice, / In fair round belly with good capon lined, / With eyes severe and beard of formal cut, / Full of wise saws and modern instances; / And so he plays his part." In the fifth stage, according to Jaques, man has achieved a career (in this case that of a judge). He has matured beyond the brashness that characterized him as a young man. But middle age seems boring; it is defined by things "formal" and commonplace and confined to the expectations implicit in his "part" as judge.

Sixth Age: "The sixth age shifts / Into the lean and slipper'd pantaloon, / With spectacles on nose and pouch on side, / His youthful hose, well saved, a world too wide / For his shrunk shank; and his big manly voice, / Turning again toward childish treble, pipes / And whistles in his sound." Aging is depicted as physical deterioration—man's eyesight fails, he loses weight, and his voice loses its depth and power.

Seventh Age: "Last scene of all, / That ends this strange eventful history, / Is second childishness and mere oblivion, / Sans teeth, sans eyes, sans taste, sans everything." Jaques describes the final age as a return to infancy because man has nothing. It is a despairing thought, since he acquired strength, vitality, money, and reputation in the preceding stages, only to lose it all in the last. And, of course, the end is "oblivion"—death.

It is interesting that as Jaques finishes his monologue on the inevitable fate of humans, Orlando enters carrying Adam—who has become weak from lack of food—like a child. Adam is now an old man, as Jaques would say, in the seventh age. Orlando's efforts show that Adam is not "sans everything" because he has someone who cares for him.

Despite Jaques's narrow perspective on the human condition, his monologue does point out how quickly humans can and do change. Change is everywhere for the characters in the Forest of Arden, even if they are unaware of it. As Shakespeare shows, they enter in one condition and leave in another. The once wicked and hate-filled Oliver now loves his brother and Celia. The villainous Frederick turns to a life of spiritual contemplation. And, of course, Rosalind brings about a change in the emotions of the love-sick Orlando. Her disguise as Ganymede—a change from woman to man—is the play's most dramatic change. Appearing as a young man, she is able to influence both her own love affair with Orlando and the intentions of the hitherto immoveable Phebe.

MOTIFS

A motif is a literary device, usually an idea or image, that recurs throughout the work to help develop the major themes of a play. Two important motifs in As You Like It are homoeroticism and exile.

Homoeroticism is the representation of same-sex love, especially as depicted in literature. However, in the plays of Shakespeare and other artists of the time, it is not understood as portraying sexual love and desire. Rather, it refers more generally to romantic, or affectionate, friendships. During the Renaissance, and well into the nineteenth century, same-sex romantic friendships were considered quite common and did not involve sexual intimacy.

Such friendships occur in many of Shakespeare's plays and poems. In As You Like It, cousins Rosalind and Celia are extremely close friends. It is even noted by the other characters. In Act I, Scene 1, wrestler Charles speaks to Oliver about the two young women:

> FOR THE DUKE'S DAUGHTER [CELIA], HER COUSIN, SO
> LOVES HER, BEING EVER
> FROM THEIR CRADLES BRED TOGETHER, THAT SHE
> WOULD HAVE FOLLOWED
> HER EXILE, OR HAVE DIED TO STAY BEHIND HER. SHE
> [ROSALIND] IS AT THE COURT,
> AND NO LESS BELOVED OF HER UNCLE THAN HIS OWN
> DAUGHTER; AND NEVER TWO
> LADIES LOVED AS THEY DO.

When Rosalind is banished from court by her uncle, Celia's father, Celia goes into exile with her: "And do not seek to take your change upon you, / To bear your griefs yourself and leave me out; / For, by this heaven, now at our sorrows pale, / Say what thou canst, 'I'll go along with thee'" (I.3). Rosalind seems not at all astonished that her cousin would leave the court with her. She says only: "Why, whither shall we go?" To the modern reader, their relationship may seem out of the ordinary, but it would not have been odd to Elizabethan audiences.

In understanding the play, it is important to understand that the relationship between Rosalind and Celia does not assume a sexual identity. It is powerful and close. It is one of the ways in which Shakespeare expounds upon the wide range of intimacy in human expression.

Another aspect of homoeroticism that delighted Elizabethan audiences is Rosalind's cross-dressing. For her assumed name, she chooses Ganymede, a well-known homoerotic figure from Greek mythology. He was the most handsome among mortals, cupbearer to the gods, and beloved of Zeus. People were drawn to Ganymede, just as Orlando is drawn to disguised Rosalind and has no problem discussing romance with what he assumes is a young lad. And Phebe, all the while scorning the attentions of Silvius, falls for Rosalind dressed as Ganymede. Once again, Shakespeare explores the vast possibilities of human attraction.

Exile is another important motif in *As You Like It*. All the action and all the romantic relationships that develop are results of the banishment of the main characters from their natural habitat. Rosalind, her father, and Orlando are unwilling exiles. Celia, Adam, and Duke Senior's loyal lords choose exile for reasons of love and loyalty. While in exile, they try to find a sense of peace in their new environment. In the end, the exiled ones return to their rightful and preferred home.

SYMBOLS

Symbols are characters, objects, or figures that stand for—and help to explain or enlarge—concepts or ideas. Two important symbols in *As You Like It* are animals and love poems.

The melancholy Jaques is convinced that the forest is no place for humans; it belongs to the animals. And, indeed, animals have an important place in the development of the plot and of the characters themselves. In Act II, Scene 1, Duke Senior asks where Jaques can be found. He is told by the First Lord that Jaques is weeping over the fallen deer in the forest, "swearing that we / Are mere usurpers, tyrants and what's worse / To fright the animals and to kill them up / In their assign'd and native dwelling-place." The Duke's men have just killed the deer for dinner, which the Duke laments but knows it is necessary for the men to eat. By Scene 5, Jaques is still mourning the dead animal and will have nothing to do with the Duke, who ordered the killing: "And I have been all this day to avoid him. He is too disputable for my company."

Animals also play an important part in Oliver's near miraculous conversion in Act IV, Scene 3. He suddenly arrives at the shepherd's cottage in the forest with a bloody handkerchief. He tells Rosalind (as Ganymede) how Orlando saved his life: Tired from his wandering in the forest, Oliver lay down to rest when a snake wrapped itself around his neck. When Orlando approached, the snake slipped under a bush. However, a lioness was laying in wait, ready to pounce if Oliver moved. Orlando saw that the sleeping man was his brother and slew the lioness. Oliver had been sent into the forest by Frederick to get rid of Orlando. Failing that, he is another exile. But Oliver realizes that this exile does not have to be a punishment. It may be a new beginning. With his newfound conversion, he rejects his villainous and evil ways. In addition, he meets Celia and immediately falls in love.

Orlando's love poems, no matter how drippy or poorly written, are also important symbols in *As You Like It*. Carving a beloved's name in trunks of trees or attaching poems to them may sound silly to modern readers, but they are common in pastoral works. In this case, Orlando, a man from the city, is imitating the shepherds. It was generally assumed that because shepherds spent their time in the natural, calm habitat of the forest, they were able to experience true love. Those caught in the intrigues of city life, however, would supposedly be more likely to experience lust. Therefore, Shakespeare is showing the audience that Orlando is experiencing true love as he decorates the forest branches with poems for Rosalind.

In his poetry, Orlando also compares Rosalind to the great heroines in fact and fiction. In Act III, Scene 2, Celia comes upon a poem in which Orlando speaks of his love in this way:

> NATURE PRESENTLY DISTILL'D
> HELEN'S CHEEK, BUT NOT HER HEART,
> CLEOPATRA'S MAJESTY,
> ATALANTA'S BETTER PART,
> SAD LUCRETIA'S MODESTY.

Helen of Troy caused the Trojan War around 1250 BCE when she was abducted by Paris. The beautiful Cleopatra ruled Egypt around 50 BCE. In Greek mythology, Atalanta was forced to kill any suitor who lost a race with her. The abduction of Lucretia, legendary chaste and modest heroine of ancient Rome, was said to have brought down the monarchy and opened the way for the republic, supposedly around 509 BCE. Orlando's message is that Rosalind has Helen's beauty (she was said to be the most beautiful woman in Greece), the regal bearing of Cleopatra, the bravery of Atalanta, and the modesty of Lucretia.

LANGUAGE

One of the common complaints from first-time readers of Shakespeare is, "I don't understand what he's talking about!" But a closer look can unlock most of the mystery. In all his plays, Shakespeare uses three forms of language. They are prose, rhymed verse, and blank verse.

Prose is writing that imitates everyday speech and has no particular rhyme pattern. Lines don't have the same number of syllables, and both upper- and lower-class characters speak in prose. Shakespeare uses it for normal conversation or descriptions of scenes and situations. In *As You Like It*, for example, in Act II, Scene 6, when Orlando and Adam first enter the Forest of Arden. Adam says he is weak from lack of food and can go no farther. In telling Adam that he will find a way to nourish him, Orlando replies in prose:

> WHY, HOW NOW, ADAM NO GREATER HEART IN THEE?
> LIVE A LITTLE; COMFORT A LITTLE; CHEER THYSELF
> A LITTLE. IF THIS UNCOUTH FOREST YIELD ANYTHING
> SAVAGE, I WILL EITHER BE FOOD FOR IT OR BRING
> IT FOR FOOD TO THEE. THY CONCEIT IS NEARER
> DEATH THAN THEY POWERS. FOR MY SAKE BE
> COMFORTABLE; HOLD DEATH AWHILE AT THE ARM'S
> END: I WILL HERE BE WITH THEE PRESENTLY; AND IF
> I BRING THEE NOT SOMETHING TO EAT, I WILL GIVE
> THEE LEAVE TO DIE: BUT IF THOU DIEST BEFORE I
> COME, THOU ART A MOCKER OF MY LABOUR.

The lower classes speak in prose as well. The shepherd Corin, in Act III, Scene 2, converses with Touchstone about manners and behavior in the court and in the country:

> NOT A WHIT, TOUCHSTONE; THOSE THAT ARE GOOD
> MANNERS AT THE COURT ARE AS RIDICULOUS IN
> THE COUNTRY AS THE BEHAVIOR OF THE COUNTRY
> IS MOST MOCKABLE AT THE COURT. YOU TOLD ME
> YOU SALUTE NOT AT THE COURT, BUT YOU KISS
> YOUR HANDS: THAT COURTESY WOULD BE
> UNCLEANLY, IF COURTIERS WERE SHEPHERDS.

For rhymed verse, the form may be two lines ending with words that rhyme or several lines with an alternating (every other line) rhyme scheme. Shakespeare often uses rhymed verse for passages that point to a moral or give advice. Rhymed verse seems to add to the imagery of the words. In Act III, Scene 2, Orlando prepares to decorate the forest with love poems for Rosalind:

> RUN, RUN, ORLANDO; CARVE ON EVERY TREE
> THE FAIR, THE CHASTE AND UNEXPRESSIVE SHE.

In Act III, Scene 4, Corin suggests that Rosalind and Celia watch Silvius as he courts the scornful Phebe. It will be a diversion, the shepherd suggests, from Rosalind's constant thoughts about Orlando. She replies:

> O, come, let us remove;
> The sight of lovers feedeth those in love.
> Bring us to this sight, and you shall say
> I'll prove a busy actor in their play.

And in Act V, Scene 4, Duke Senior welcomes the wedding couples with:

> O my dear niece, welcome thou art to me!
> Even daughter, welcome, in no less degree.

Duke Senior concludes the scene, and the last act, with:

> Proceed, proceed: we will begin these rites,
> As we do trust they'll end, in true delights.

"I PRAY YOU DO NOT FALL IN LOVE WITH ME."

Note that in rhymed verse, unlike prose, the first words of every line are capitalized.

Shakespeare often uses blank verse, which comes close to the natural rhythms of spoken English, for passionate or momentous occasions, such as Hamlet's "To be, or not to be" speech. Blank verse is unrhymed iambic pentameter, which means that lines have ten syllables with a recognizable meter. The ten syllables in the lines alternate between unstressed and stressed syllables. To distinguish blank verse from prose, read it aloud. A regular pattern of "da DUM da DUM da DUM da DUM da DUM" indicates blank verse. Though there is no regular pattern of end-of-line rhyme, occasionally a couple of lines do rhyme. Like rhymed verse, the first word of each line is capitalized.

In Act I, Scene 2, Le Beau warns Orlando to leave the palace after he has defeated Charles in the wrestling match and disgraced Duke Frederick:

> GOOD SIR, I DO IN FRIENDSHIP COUNSEL YOU
> TO LEAVE THIS PLACE. ALBEIT YOU HAVE DESERVED
> HIGH COMMENDATION, TRUE APPLAUSE AND LOVE,
> YET SUCH IS NOW THE DUKE'S CONDITION
> THAT HE MISCONSTRUES ALL THAT YOU HAVE DONE.
> THE DUKE IS HUMOROUS: WHAT HE IS INDEED,
> MORE SUITS YOU TO CONCEIVE THAN I TO SPEAK OF.

In Act I, Scene 3, when Rosalind has been exiled, Celia uses blank verse to speak passionately about what they should do:

> NO, HATH NOT? ROSALIND LACKS THEN THE LOVE
> THAT TEACHETH THEE THAT THOU AND I AM ONE:
> SHALL WE BE SUNDER'D? SHALL WE PART, SWEET GIRL?
> NO: LET MY FATHER SEEK ANOTHER HEIR.
> THEREFORE DEVISE WITH ME HOW WE MAY FLY,
> WHITHER TO GO AND WHAT TO BEAR WITH US;
> AND DO NOT SEEK TO TAKE YOUR CHANGE UPON YOU,
> TO BEAR YOUR GRIEFS YOURSELF AND LEAVE ME OUT;
> FOR, BY THIS HEAVEN, NOW AT OUR SORROWS PALE,
> SAY WHAT THOU CANST, I'LL GO ALONG WITH THEE.

As You Like It is primarily written in prose with very little plot. The characters move into the forest and out again. When the romantic plots begin, the characters speak in verse, especially Rosalind and Orlando as they fall in love. But conversation between Rosalind and Celia remains in prose. In Act II, Scene 4, Rosalind, Celia, and Touchstone carry on their conversations in prose. When the shepherds—Corin and Silvius—enter, as they speak of pastoral love, they speak in verse.

Some scholars say that the pastoral poetry of *As You Like It* demands knowledge of Elizabethan culture more than in most of Shakespeare's works. There are comments throughout on the pros and cons of city and country life. Fashions of both court and country are mocked by the characters. Through most of the play, different characters in the forest randomly meet each other. Shakespeare incorporates these chance meetings because the conversations between unlike characters present the audience with different attitudes about life and love.

For full enjoyment, it would seem an advantage if the spectator can distinguish between all these suggestions. It may be true that much of the interest and fun in *As You Like It* comes from styles, beliefs, and mores that were of another time. But the modern audience can still identify with the lovesick Orlando and his tree-trunk carvings or the amusement of Rosalind over his bad poetry. For most readers, the comic delights of the play outweigh anything that is passé.

INTERPRETING THE PLAY

The rich and varied romanticism of *As You Like It* gave it much popularity. This was especially true during the changing attitudes of the Victorian era. Most all theater seasons included a staging of the play, especially in the last half of the nineteenth century. But after World War II, revivals became less frequent, although it was still popular with college groups. Revivals continue today, often with variations. That includes a 2005 Stratford Festival production in Ontario, Canada, that set the comedy in the 1960s, and a 2007 production in New York set in the Old West.

Shakespeare was a unique writer of comedies, and is considered one of the best English playwrights of all time. His comedies are chiefly admired because they are so rich in humor and so delightful in their exploration of the human experience. *As You Like It* transports the reader or viewer out of the actual world into a place of dreams. And in that place—in this case, the Forest of Arden—the characters act in a variety of ways. Don't look for deep social philosophy in this play. It is meant to be enjoyed and savored for what it is—a rich tapestry of human emotions. Shakespeare had great insight into different stages of life. He well understood the varied reactions to human experiences.

As You Like It is the sunniest of plays, the merriest of comedies. Its richness relies on two striking features. For one, the Forest of Arden is a nearly mythical place of charm, a haven from the perils of human existence. And in that haven, the characters beneath the canopy of trees are free to roam at will. They are free to speak their minds with whom they chance to meet. And, most of all, they are free to fall in love at first sight.

In addition, the improbable plays a large role in the comedy. Such happenings as sudden conversions from evil to good are all part of the plot. The characters exist in a world in which brother hates brother and one is willing to inflict the other with great harm, even death. But when the exiled characters are in the forest, their world is an enemy-less haven where problems seem to evaporate in easy solutions.

Audiences accept all these improbable changes of mood and action and delight in them. These separate parts form a unity that is part of the attraction. From Shakespeare's day and into modern times, *As You Like It* draws the viewer under its spell.

Staging a play such as this comedy in Elizabethan times was a less complicated affair than today. Instead of having to worry about the many shifts of scenes, the actors simply entered the stage and began speaking, with little changes in background or props.

Most of *As You Like It* is given over to fun and silly situations. Yet for all the silliness of love, for all the love poems on trees, the characters actually do discuss more serious ideas, such as the meaning of love and life. It is this mixing of dramatic conversation with a healthy dose of comedy that has made the play appeal to audiences for centuries.

In 1723, *As You Like It* was performed in the Drury Lane theater in London, staged by Charles Johnson. It was the first of many significantly altered versions. Adaptations of Shakespeare's plays were common and popular in the eighteenth and nineteenth centuries. They helped to

"LOVE HIM; HE WORSHIPS YOU."

"THESE TREES SHALL BE MY BOOKS."

keep up the interest in his works. Johnson, a tavern keeper as well as a playwright, called his adaptation *Love in a Forest*. It was presented without the characters of court jester Touchstone and several of the country people. In Johnson's version, Jaques, not Oliver, falls in love with Celia. And instead of a wrestling match between Charles and Orlando, the two have a duel with swords.

Shakespeare's original version was performed in 1740 at Drury Lane. Since that time, there have been many fine productions of *As You Like It*. The two most notable were staged at London's Old Vic Theater in 1936 starring Edith Evans and at the Shakespeare Memorial Theater in Stratford-upon-Avon, Shakespeare's birthplace, in 1961. That version starred Vanessa Redgrave, who was born into a well-known family of actors in London. The longest-running Broadway production opened in 1950 with film star Katharine Hepburn as Rosalind opposite William Prince as Orlando. It ran for 145 performances.

Famed English actor Laurence Olivier starred in *As You Like It*, his first Shakespeare film, made in the United Kingdom in 1936. It also starred the director's wife, Elisabeth Bergner, who played Rosalind with a thick German accent. The movie did not get good reviews. The National Theater Company of Great Britain staged an unusual (for modern times) production in 1967 with an all-male cast. It toured the United States and played in New York City in 1974.

Three years later, the Royal Shakespeare Company also produced an unusual version. It was set in the Forest of Arden in a bitter winter with icicles hanging from the trees. The next year, the English actress Helen Mirren played Rosalind in a BBC production. In 2006, director Kenneth Branagh released his version of the play, set in nineteenth-century Japan. Made for the big screen, it was released only to theaters in Europe and aired on HBO in the United States in 2007.

According to Minnesota radio station WCAL, *As You Like It* may have been the first play ever to go on the air. It was broadcast in 1922.

 TONE

The tone of a play refers to how things are said or done, not what. It comes from the symbols, the language, the images that are presented; in other words, what makes up the play. There are really only two changes of tone in *As You Like It*. The first two scenes of Act I and Act II, as well as the first scene of Act III, are set at court. They are charged with anger and villainy as both Oliver and Duke Frederick try to rid themselves of brothers. The rest of the play is set in Arden where, in contrast, life is filled with serenity, overwhelming love sickness, and endless, often witty, conversation.

Chronology

1564 William Shakespeare is born on April 23 in Stratford-upon-Avon, England

1578–1582 Span of Shakespeare's "Lost Years," covering the time between leaving school and marrying Anne Hathaway of Stratford

1582 At age eighteen Shakespeare marries Anne Hathaway, age twenty-six, on November 28

1583 Susanna Shakespeare, William and Anne's first child, is born in May, six months after the wedding

1584 Birth of twins Hamnet and Judith Shakespeare

1585–1592 Shakespeare leaves his family in Stratford to become an actor and playwright in a London theater company

1587 Public beheading of Mary, Queen of Scots

1593–1594 The Bubonic (Black) Plague closes theaters in London

1594–1596 As a leading playwright, Shakespeare creates some of his most popular work, including *A Midsummer Night's Dream* and *Romeo and Juliet*

1596 Hamnet Shakespeare dies in August at age eleven, possibly of plague

1596–1597	*The Merchant of Venice* and *Henry IV, Part One*, most likely are written
1599	The Globe Theater opens
1600	*Julius Caesar* is first performed at the Globe
1600–1601	*Hamlet* is believed to have been written
1601–1602	*Twelfth Night* is probably composed
1603	Queen Elizabeth dies; Scottish king James VI succeeds her and becomes England's James I
1604	Shakespeare pens *Othello*
1605	*Macbeth* is composed
1608–1610	London's theaters are forced to close when the plague returns and kills an estimated 33,000 people
1611	*The Tempest* is written
1613	The Globe Theater is destroyed by fire
1614	Reopening of the Globe
1616	Shakespeare dies on April 23
1623	Anne Hathaway, Shakespeare's widow, dies; a collection of Shakespeare's plays, known as the First Folio, is published

Source Notes

p. 41, par. 2, In this play, Rosalind dresses as a man for safety while traveling. But Shakespeare was not above exploiting his audiences' interest in such conventions as cross-dressing. In *Twelfth Night*, for instance, Viola turns herself into handsome Cesario to break the heart of Countess Olivia. Because the audience is aware of the deception, they are amused by it. They were all the more delighted because at the time, women were not allowed on stage, so female roles were played by young men. Thus there was a boy playing a woman disguised as a man. It was all great fun to the Elizabethans.

p. 42, par. 1, Touchstone is one of Shakespeare's most witty jesters. The history of jesters at court traces back to the Middle Ages. They may not have been important historically, but they certainly did liven up court life. Mainly, they were charged with bringing a smile to a monarch who was depressed or ill. Very early court jesters dressed much like circus clowns. This evolved into gaudy, colorful costumes complete with a distinctive three-pointed cloth hat that had a jingle bell at the end of each point. During the reign of Elizabeth I (1558–1603), the court jester was usually also an actor. Among the most famous are Richard Tarlton, jester, actor, and playwright for the queen, and Robert Armin (1568–1615), who was also a principal actor in Shakespeare's plays. There were also some female court jesters, including Lucretia the Tumbler and Jane the Fool. In addition to Touchstone in *As You Like It*, Shakespeare used jesters in many of his other plays, such as the clown in Othello or Puck in *A Midsummer Night's Dream*.

p. 71, par. 1, The word cuckold is from the Old French for "cuckoo," and dates from the Middle Ages. It refers to a man whose wife has romantic affairs of which he is unaware. Everyone else knows but him or, in other words, he is wearing horns that only he cannot see. It is said that some European communities gathered to humiliate a man whose wife had given birth to a child that did not look like him. He was required to parade through town with antlers on his head. Cuckold is one of the few masculine words in the English language that does not have a feminine counterpart.

p. 76, par. 5–p. 77, par. 1, Music plays an important role in this Shakespeare comedy, especially in Act V, scene 4, when Hymen, the god of marriage, is present for the wedding of the four couples. The music creates a spectacle, which draws the audience into believing that all these unions take place in a rational, believable manner. When Rosalind's epilogue follows, the music is absent, perhaps to bring the audience back to reality. In all, the play contains seven songs (five were original and two were added in 1740), including "Blow, blow thou winter wind," "Under the greenwood tree," and "It was a lover and his lass." They aid the plot in producing a woodland atmosphere, especially when the play is staged inside with minimal scenery.

A Shakespeare Glossary

The student should not try to memorize these, but only refer to them as needed. We can never stress enough that the best way to learn Shakespeare's language is simply to *hear* it—to hear it spoken well by good actors. After all, small children master every language on Earth through their ears, without studying dictionaries, and we should master Shakespeare, as much as possible, the same way.

addition — a name or title (knight, duke, duchess, king, etc.)
admire — to marvel
affect — to like or love; to be attracted to
an — if ("An I tell you that, I'll be hanged.")
approve — to prove or confirm
attend — to pay attention
belike — probably
beseech — to beg or request
betimes — soon; early
bondman — a slave
bootless — futile; useless; in vain
broil — a battle
charge — expense, responsibility; to command or accuse
clepe, clept — to name; named
common — of the common people; below the nobility
conceit — imagination
condition — social rank; quality
countenance — face; appearance; favor
cousin — a relative
cry you mercy — beg your pardon
curious — careful; attentive to detail
dear — expensive
discourse — to converse; conversation
discover — to reveal or uncover
dispatch — to speed or hurry; to send; to kill
doubt — to suspect

entreat — to beg or appeal

envy — to hate or resent; hatred; resentment

ere — before

ever, e'er — always

eyne — eyes

fain — gladly

fare — to eat; to prosper

favor — face, privilege

fellow — a peer or equal

filial — of a child toward his or her parent

fine — an end; "in fine" = in sum

fond — foolish

fool — a darling

genius — a good or evil spirit

gentle — well-bred; not common

gentleman — one whose labor was done by servants (Note: to call someone a *gentleman* was not a mere compliment on his manners; it meant that he was above the common people.)

gentles — people of quality

get — to beget (a child)

go to — "go on"; "come off it"

go we — let us go

haply — perhaps

happily — by chance; fortunately

hard by — nearby

heavy — sad or serious

husbandry — thrift; economy

instant — immediate

kind — one's nature; species

knave — a villain; a poor man

lady — a woman of high social rank (Note: *lady* was not a synonym for *woman* or *polite woman*; it was not a compliment, but, like *gentleman*, simply a word referring to one's actual legal status in society.)

leave — permission; "take my leave" = depart (with permission)

lief, lieve — "I had as lief" = I would just as soon; I would rather

like — to please; "it likes me not" = it is disagreeable to me

livery — the uniform of a nobleman's servants; emblem
mark — notice; pay attention
morrow — morning
needs — necessarily
nice — too fussy or fastidious
owe — to own
passing — very
peculiar — individual; exclusive
privy — private; secret
proper — handsome; one's very own ("his proper son")
protest — to insist or declare
quite — completely
require — request
several — different; various
severally — separately
sirrah — a term used to address social inferiors
sooth — truth
state — condition; social rank
still — always; persistently
success — result(s)
surfeit — fullness
touching — concerning; about; as for
translate — to transform
unfold — to disclose
villain — a low or evil person; originally, a peasant
voice — a vote; consent; approval
vouchsafe — to confide or grant
vulgar — common
want — to lack
weeds — clothing
what ho — "hello, there!"
wherefore — why
wit — intelligence; sanity
withal — moreover; nevertheless
without — outside
would — wish

Suggested Essay Topics

1. Who do you think is the more villainous character—Oliver for wanting to harm his brother Orlando, or Frederick for exiling his brother Duke Senior? Why?

2. Do you think it is likely that Orlando had a suspicion that Ganymede was really Rosalind? Explain your answer.

3. In this comedy, the characters often compare the benefits of country versus city living. What do you think are the benefits or disadvantages of both in the twenty-first century?

4. Do you find it believable that Oliver would suddenly change from hating his brother to loving his brother after Orlando rescues him? Give your reasons why.

5. Who do you think is the stronger personality in the play—Rosalind or Orlando? Explain your answer.

Testing Your Memory

1. This play is known as a: a) tragedy; b) historical drama; c) pastoral comedy; d) sonnet

2. This play is based on a prose romance by Thomas Lodge called: a) Rosemary; b) Celia; c) Rosalynde; d) Rose

3. The Forest of Arden may describe what ancient woodland? a) Ardennes in France and Belgium; b) Ardennes in Germany; c) Ardennes in Italy; d) Ardennes in Sweden

4. Primogeniture is a practice in which: a) the oldest son inherits the wealth; b) the youngest son inherits the wealth; c) the oldest daughter inherits the wealth; d) nobody inherits the wealth

5. As the play opens, why is Orlando so angry with his brother Oliver? a) Oliver doesn't give him spending money; b) Oliver won't pay for his education; c) Oliver has stolen his girl; d) Oliver won't let him wrestle

6. Why is Duke Senior living in the Forest of Arden? a) His brother Frederick exiled him; b) He hates court life; c) He is ill; d) Judges at court asked him to leave

7. Who is Celia's father? a) Duke Senior; b) Touchstone; c) Jaques; d) Duke Frederick

8. Why does Duke Frederick exile Rosalind? a) She does not speak politely to him; b) She is rude to his daughter; c) She is in love with Orlando; d) She is her father's daughter

9. Why does Rosalind disguise herself as Ganymede? a) For protection when traveling; b) To hide from Duke Frederick; c) To hide from her father; d) For laughs

10. What word best describes the character of Jaques? a) truthful; b) testy; c) melancholy; d) sarcastic

11. Why is Jaques so upset with Duke Senior after the hunt? a) Jaques was not invited to the feast; b) Jaques was not invited to the hunt; c) A deer was killed; d) One of the lords was killed

12. Celia disguises herself as a: a) page; b) shepherdess; c) boy; d) animal

13. In Jaques's "All the world's a stage" speech, what are men and women? a) bad players; b) helpless players; c) unwilling players; d) merely players

14. What does Orlando carve on tree trunks? a) Rosalind's name; b) love letters; c) his name; d) Ganymede's name

15. Who would have played the roles of Rosalind or Celia in Elizabethan times? a) young women; b) boys; c) older women; d) older men

16. What makes Audrey such an odd mate for the witty Touchstone? a) She is sharp witted; b) She is twice his age; c) She is dull witted; d) She does not love him

17. At the end of the play, Celia marries: a) William; b) Touchstone; c) Oliver; d) Duke Senior

18. What happens when Rosalind (as Ganymede) learns that Orlando has been wounded by a lioness? a) She cries; b) She goes to rescue him; c) She forgets him; d) She faints

19. What is the relationship of Jaques du Boys to Orlando? a) older brother; b) friend; c) younger brother; d) cousin

20. Who delivers the Epilogue? a) Orlando; b) Rosalind; c) Celia; d) Audrey

Answer Key

12. b; 13. d; 14. a; 15. b; 16. c; 17. c; 18. d; 19. a; 20. b

1. c; 2. c; 3. a; 4. a; 5. b; 6. a; 7. d; 8. d; 9. a; 10. c; 11. c;

Further Information

BOOKS

As You Like It. The New Cambridge Shakespeare. Edited by Michael Hattaway. New York: Cambridge University Press, 2000.

As You Like It. Folger Shakespeare Library. Edited by Barbara A. Mowat and Paul Werstine. New York: Washington Square Press, 2004.

As You Like It. Manga Shakespeare. Adapted by Richard Appignanesi. New York: Harry N. Abrams/Amulet, 2009.

WEBSITES

http://absoluteshakespeare.com
Absolute Shakespeare is a resource for the Bard's plays, sonnets, and poems and includes summaries, quotes, films, trivia, and more.

www.playshakespeare.com
Play Shakespeare features all the play texts with an online glossary, reviews, a discussion forum, and links to festivals worldwide.

www.william-shakespeare.info/shakespeare-play-as-you-like-it.htm
William Shakespeare: The Complete Works provides links related to the specific plays, as well as articles about Shakespeare's life, world, and works.

Bibliography

William Shakespeare

Bate, Jonathan, and Eric Rasmussen. *William Shakespeare: The Complete Works*. New York: Modern Library, 2007.

Bloom, Harold. *Shakespeare: The Invention of the Human*. New York: Riverhead, 1998.

Cahn, Victor L. *The Plays of Shakespeare: A Thematic Guide*. Westport, CT: Greenwood, 2001.

Dunton-Downer, Leslie, and Alan Riding. *The Essential Shakespeare Handbook*. New York: DK, 2004.

Fallon, Robert Thomas. *A Theatergoer's Guide to Shakespeare*. Chicago: Ivan R. Dee, 2001.

———. *A Theatergoer's Guide to Shakespeare's Characters*. Chicago: Ivan R. Dee, 2004.

———. *A Theatergoer's Guide to Shakespeare's Themes*. Chicago: Ivan R. Dee, 2002.

Frye, Roland Mushat. *Shakespeare's Life and Times*. Princeton, NJ: Princeton University Press, 1975.

Kermode, Frank. *Shakespeare's Language*. New York: Farrar, 2000.

McLeish, Kenneth. *Shakespeare's Characters*. Studio City, CA: Players Press, 1992.

Ornstein, Robert. *Shakespeare's Comedies: From Roman Farce to Romantic Mystery*. Newark, NJ: University of Delaware, 1986.

Vaughn, Jack A. *Shakespeare's Comedies*. New York: Ungar, 1980.

As You Like It

Clark, William George, and William Aldis Wright. *The Complete Works of William Shakespeare*. New York: Grosset & Dunlap, 1911.

Hattaway, Michael, ed. *As You Like It*. Cambridge, UK: Cambridge University Press, 2000.

Index

Page numbers in **boldface** are illustrations.

a

Act I
    scene 1, 46–48
    scene 2, 49–52
    scene 3, 52–53
Act II
    scene 1, 53–54
    scene 2, 54–55
    scene 3, 55
    scene 4, 56–57
    scene 5, 58
    scene 6, 58–59
    scene 7, 59–60
Act III
    scene 1, 60–61
    scene 2, 61–63
    scene 3, 64–66
    scene 4, 66–67
    scene 5, 67–68
Act IV
    scene 1, 68–70
    scene 2, 70–71
    scene 3, 71–72
Act V
    scene 1, 72–74
    scene 2, 74–75
    scene 3, 75–76
    scene 4, 76–78
actors, 23
All's Well That Ends Well, 72

A Midsummer Night's Dream, 5
A Midsummer Night's Dream (movie), 16
Antony and Cleopatra, 31
Arden, Mary, 43
As You Like It (movie), 13, **39**, **45**

B

Bacon, Francis, 26
Bannen, Ian, **97**
Bates, Paul, **73**
bearbaiting, 21
blank verse, 106–107
Borrelli, Michael, **93**
Branagh, Kenneth, 13
Burbage, Richard, 12

C

Carmichael, Clark, **57**
Celia, **64**, 87
Censorship, 23
characters, 80–87
chronology, 112–113
comedies, 40, 108
Coriolanus, 31
Crane, Ralph, 40
critics, 42

D

de Vere, Edward, Earl of Oxford, 27
disguise, 52–53, 56, 63, 66, 68, 70, 72, 75, 76–77, 81–82, 100, 101

E

Elizabeth I, 11, **20**, 20–21, 25, 30
entertainment, 21
epilogue, 78–79

F

Fiennes, Joseph, **29**
films, 13–19
folio, 33

G

Globe Theater, 22, **22**
groundlings, 21

H

Hamlet, 5
Hamlet, 30
Hamlet (movie), 13–14
Hathaway, Anne, 12
Health issues, 20
Henry IV, 28
Henry IV, Part One (movie), 14
Henry VIII, 11
human experience, stages of, 96, 98–100

I

interpretation, 108–111

J

James I, 30
James VI, 30
Jaques, **57**, 84, **85**, 86
Johnson, Stephen Paul, **73**
Jonson, Ben, 33

Julius Caesar, 29–30
Julius Caesar (movie), 15

K

Kay, Barnaby, **49**, **79**
King Henry VI, 25
King Lear, 31
King Lear (movie), 15
King's Men, 30–31

L

language
    famous quotes, 5, 9
    literary terms, 34–37
    Shakespeare glossary, 116–118
    Shakespeare's, 6–10, 104–107
Lodge, Thomas, 42
Lord Chamberlain's Men, 12, 30–31
love poems, 61–63, **64**, **79**, 83, 94, 103
love, nature of, 92–96

M

Macbeth, 31
Macbeth (movie), 15
Marcell, Joseph, **85**
Marlowe, Christopher, 27
McGloin, Matthew, **85**
The Merchant of Venice (movie), 16
Meres, Francis, 28–29
motifs, 100–101
movies, 13–19
Mr. William Shakespeares Comedies, Histories, & Tragedies (folio), 33, 40
Mudek, Valeri, **93**

Index

Page numbers in **boldface** are illustrations.

O

Orlando, **49**, **79**, 82–84
Othello, 31
Othello (movie), 16–17
overview, 40–43

P

pastoral comedy, 41
plays, 25–30
prose, 104–105
Puritans, 21, 23–24

Q

Quaid, Amanda, **64**

R

The Rape of Lucrece, 12
Redgrave, Vanessa, **97**
religious conflict, 10–11, 20–21, 23–24
Reynolds, Jon, **85**
rhymed verse, 105–106
Richard II, 28
Richard III, 25
Richard III (movie), 17
Romeo and Juliet, 28
Romeo and Juliet (movie), 17–18
Rosalind, **64**, **79**, 81–82
Rosalynde, 42
Royal Shakespeare Theater, **24**

S

Seven Ages of Man, 84, 96, 98–99
Shakespeare, John (father), 10
Shakespeare, William
    childhood home, **11**
    children, 12, 28
    chronology, 112–113
    death, 31–32
    doubts about authorship, 26–27
    early life, 10–12
    marriage, 12
    reputation, 4, 30–31, 33
    retirement, 31–32
    tombstone, 32, **32**
Shakespeare In Love, **29**
Silverman, Miriam, **64**
society, Shakespeare's, 20–24
sonnets, 31
symbols, 102–103

T

The Taming of the Shrew, 25, 28
The Taming of the Shrew (movie), 18
The Tempest, 31
The Tempest (movie), 18
Ten Things I Hate About You (movie), 25, 28
theater productions, 21–25
theaters, 21–22, **22**, **24**
themes, 90–100

city life v. country life, 58, 61, 65–66,
74, 78, 90–92

nature of love, 82, 87, 92–96 stages of
human experience, 60, 96, 98–100

timeline, 112–113

tone, 111

Touchstone, **73**, 86–87

Twelfth Night (movie), 19

Vazquez, Ricardo, **57**

Venus and Adonis, 12

Wars of the Roses, 25

West Side Story (movie), 28

Williams, Lia, **79**

Williamson, Nance, **57**

Wriothesley, Henry, Earl of Southampton,
12

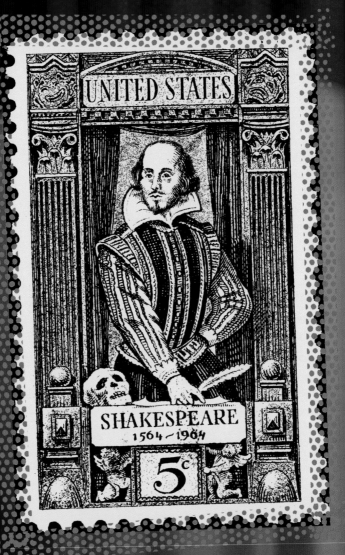

About the Author

A former children's book editor and U.S. Navy journalist, Corinne J. Naden has written more than ninety books for children and young adults, including *Romeo and Juliet* and *The Taming of the Shrew* in this series. She lives in Tarrytown, New York.